*Sweet Maria's*

# CAKE
# KITCHEN

ST. MARTIN'S GRIFFIN ∞ NEW YORK

*Sweet Maria's*

# CAKE

# KITCHEN

*Casual and Creative Recipes for Layer,
Loaf, and Bundt Cakes*

MARIA BRUSCINO SANCHEZ

ALSO BY MARIA BRUSCINO SANCHEZ

*Sweet Maria's Italian Cookie Tray*

Book design by Gretchen Achilles
Illustrations by Lizzy Rockwell

Library of Congress Cataloging-in-Publication Data

Sanchez, Maria Bruscino.
Sweet Maria's cake kitchen : casual and creative recipes for layer, loaf, and bundt cakes
/ Maria Bruscino Sanchez. — 1st St. Martin's Griffin ed.
p.      cm
Includes index.
ISBN 0-312-19527-3
1. Cake.   2. Sweet Maria's (Bakery)   I. Title.
TX771.S22 1998

641.8'653—dc21                                                                                          98-22881
                                                                                                                          CPI

First St. Martin's Griffin Edition: September 1998

10   9   8   7   6   5   4   3   2   1

FOR MY CUSTOMERS,
WHO CONTINUE TO ENCOURAGE
AND CHALLENGE ME

# CONTENTS

# ACKNOWLEDGMENTS

Many thanks to my agent, Carla Glasser, for everything.

To my editor, Marian Lizzi, and everyone at St. Martin's whose expertise has made my cookbook career an enjoyable experience.

To Mom, Dad, and Edgar for their love and patience.

To the Sweet Maria's staff for their support and encouragement.

And to Tony, Louise, and Helen, who were the first to nurture my fascination with cakes.

# INTRODUCTION

At Sweet Maria's, just about every cake order marks a birthday, a homecoming, a new baby, the union of two people, or some other celebration. It's great to be part of such a happy business, creating cakes that make someone feel special, even if it's simply to say "I love you," "TGIF," or "Happy Spring."

Today's cake has evolved from being a mere dessert to being the centerpiece of a party. At Sweet Maria's we have many requests for unusual shapes, colors, and inscriptions that either blend with or are the theme of the party. I've actually had a few customers pick out their cake first and then plan their theme and decorations around the cake.

Many people are intimidated by the thought of baking their own cakes, and not without reason. Cake baking is a science, exact in its measurements, unforgiving when it comes to miscalculations. In cooking or cookie baking, there is less that can go wrong. There are a lot of variables in cake baking: accurate measurement, fresh ingredients, the right oven temperature. But don't let that deter you. With a few tips and attention to detail you can bake and enjoy successful cakes.

This book offers a selection of some of my personal favorites and some of our biggest-selling cakes. It includes butter-based cakes as well as lighter sponge-type cakes. In Connecticut, where Sweet Maria's is located, there seems to be a regional preference for whipped cream–frosted cakes, so I've included a number of them. These cakes are usually paired with fresh fruit and offer a less sweet alternative to traditional buttercream cakes. Buttercreams are rich and sweet and are commonly used on birthday and wedding cakes. I've included these as well.

Most of the cakes in this book are made the same way we prepare them at Sweet Maria's. Of course, we bake much larger batches of both cake and frosting.

Sometimes the quality of ingredients available to bakeries is much higher than that available to the customer. For example, pasteurized heavy cream, which is the freshest, is available to us in large quantities directly through a dairy. The same dairy will sell heavy cream to a supermarket. However, they will sell them only ultra-pasteurized cream, because it has a longer shelf life. In this respect, the cakes you make may differ from those made at our bakery.

The other way they may differ is in the number of layers in the layer cakes. Most cakes frosted with whipped cream made at the bakery are three layers. We slice two layers in half horizontally to make four thin layers. We use three layers for one cake and save the odd piece for use in another cake. When you're baking at home, this would be wasteful, so I've made many of the cakes in this book into four-layer versions for the home baker.

When I was a child, my mom made all our special-occasion cakes. Every birthday, she'd make a devil's food cake with chocolate pudding frosting. It didn't have any fancy decorations—just a few swirls in the frosting. But it's always been my favorite. I hope the cakes in this book help bring the same sweet pleasure to your home.

# BEFORE YOU BEGIN

## INGREDIENTS

It is important that your cake ingredients are at room temperature. This is the only way for all the elements to blend together successfully. This makes cake baking a planned event: You must get organized and let the refrigerated ingredients come to room temperature before mixing. This usually takes two to three hours.

**FLOUR:** Cake flour is the best flour to use for most cake baking. It produces a light texture. Other flours have more gluten, which will toughen the cake. All–purpose flour and unbleached flour contain more gluten than cake flour, strengthening the batter. This type of heavier, denser batter is used primarily in fruitcakes. The higher gluten is needed to hold up the fruit and nuts and to keep them from sinking to the bottom of the cake.

**SUGAR:** Extra-fine granulated sugar is used in the cake recipes in this book. It provides a great flavor, and it blends well with butters and shortenings.

**BROWN SUGAR:** Brown sugar is sugar that has been processed with molasses for a rich flavor. You can use light brown or dark brown sugar depending on your personal preference, unless a particular type has been specified. When measuring brown sugar, spoon sugar into a measuring cup and lightly pack it into cup with the back of a spoon or with your fingers.

**CONFECTIONERS' SUGAR:** Confectioners' sugar is very fine powdered sugar that has a bit of cornstarch added to prevent sticking. Because of its fine texture, it blends well with other ingredients to produce smooth icings and glazes.

**BUTTER:** Unsalted butter is used in these recipes. It offers the fullest and freshest flavor. It's easier to add salt to your recipe as needed instead of assuming there's enough in salted butter. You can substitute margarine or shortening in these recipes, but you'll be sacrificing the fresh, full flavor of butter.

**VEGETABLE SHORTENING AND VEGETABLE OIL:** Whenever shortening is called for in these recipes, use vegetable shortening. Vegetable shortening provides a smooth texture. It can be used to grease cake pans if you're going to grease and flour them to prevent the cake from sticking in the pan.

When a recipe calls for oil, use a vegetable oil. Olive oil is very expensive and often too heavy for most cake baking.

**EXTRACTS:** Be sure to use pure extracts in all your baking. You can really taste the difference compared with cheaper flavorings. You can keep your frostings white by using a clear extract.

**EGGS:** Whole, large grade A eggs are recommended for these recipes. If you need to separate eggs, it's easier to do when they are cold. Then let the eggs come to room temperature before using.

**BAKING POWDER AND BAKING SODA:** These are two leavening agents that are commonly used in cake baking. Be sure that your supply is fresh for best results. Store unused baking powder and baking soda in airtight containers.

**MILK AND BUTTERMILK:** When a recipe calls for milk, use whole Grade A milk. Don't substitute low-fat or nonfat milk. You'll be compromising the texture and flavor of your cake.

Years ago, buttermilk was the liquid that was left after churning butter. Today it is made by adding a bacteria to whole milk to produce a slightly sour taste. It adds a richer flavor to many of our cakes.

**SPICES:** There are several common spices used in this cookbook. They include cinnamon, nutmeg, ginger, and cloves. These are readily available in supermarkets, already ground. Just be sure your supply of spices is fresh. If your spice jars have been opened for more than six months, you should replace them with a new supply.

**FRUITS AND VEGETABLES:** This book includes some cakes that require fresh fruits or vegetables. Try to take advantage of local produce and use the seasonal specialties of your area. Strawberries, raspberries, and blueberries are best when they're fresh and in season, but a good alternative is "IQF" berries. These are berries that are "individually quick frozen" separately, then frozen together. This allows the whole berry to thaw whole instead of the pieces and juice that come with other types of frozen fruits.

Every baker has his or her favorite variety of apples. Use your favorite or try Empire or Cortland. These are firm and flavorful for most baking purposes.

Pears are gaining in popularity for baking purposes and rightly so. Bosc pears bake wonderfully and are available just about all year.

**CHOCOLATE:** Always use the finest and freshest chocolate available. Most of these recipes use semisweet bars or semisweet chocolate chips that are available in most supermarkets.

**COCOA:** Many bakers will debate the best type of cocoa. I've found that Dutch-processed cocoa can't be beat for a full rich flavor and color.

**CITRUS RIND AND JUICE:** A great way to flavor cakes is by using the rind and juice of citrus fruit such as lemons, limes, and oranges. This adds a much more pungent and natural flavor than any extract. It's easier to squeeze the fruits for juice if they are at room temperature. To grate the rind, use a zester or four-sided grater. Just be sure to avoid the bitter white pith underneath the rind.

**WHIPPED CREAM:** Heavy cream is recommended for whipped cream frosting. It has a higher butterfat content than whipping cream or light cream, so it whips up the stiffest and has the richest flavor. Pasteurized heavy cream is the freshest-tasting cream, but is usually hard to find. Most supermarkets stock ultra-pasteurized cream that will work in most recipes.

**MASCARPONE:** This is a soft Italian cheese similar to cream cheese in texture. It is the basis for the Italian dessert tiramisù.

**CREAM CHEESE:** Any brand of cream cheese will work in these recipes. Be sure it is softened to room temperature for the easiest blending. Neufchatel cheese is a natural low-calorie alternative to cream cheese. It has a lower milkfat content than traditional cream cheese, and it makes a fine substitute.

**YOGURT AND SOUR CREAM:** Both yogurt and sour cream are added for flavor and moisture in some of the cakes in this book.

**NUTS:** A wide variety of nuts is used in this book, including walnuts, pecans, and almonds. In many of the recipes you can interchange the types of nuts (e.g., if the recipe calls for almonds, change to hazelnuts). If you have a large amount of nuts that you need to store, place in a plastic bag and freeze for later use.

Freshly chopping nuts helps to bring out their natural flavors and oils. This book uses various sizes of nuts.

For finely chopped, use a food processor. For coarsely chopped, use a long knife and cutting board.

Roasting nuts and coconut helps to draw out their natural oils and flavor. Lay the measured amount of nuts or coconut on a clean parchment-lined cookie sheet. Spread in a single layer. Bake in the oven at 350°F for 5 to 8 minutes, or until lightly browned. Let cool before using.

## EQUIPMENT

It is very important to have the right tools for cake baking. The wrong size pan or cheap foil layer cake pans can ruin the best batters.

**LAYER CAKE PANS:** If you are using round layer cake pans, use the ones with straight sides, two inches deep. For layer cakes, you only need the pan to be the same height as the finished cake will be. Disposable foil pans are not recommended for layer cake baking.

**LOAF PANS:** Loaf pans come in many sizes, the most common are 10 x 6 x 2½ inches and 8 x 4 x 3 inches. Foil pans are fine for loaf pans and are especially practical for wrapping and gift giving. Mini loaf pans make a unique individual dessert. These pans usually come in a set of six pans, 4½ x 2½ x 1½ inches each.

**BUNDT AND TUBE PANS:** Tube pans are round, tall pans that have a center column. Bundt was originally the brand name for a fancier fluted tube pan. Now any fluted tube pan is referred to as a Bundt pan, regardless of the manufacturer. The most common sizes are 9 x 4 inches and 10 x 4 inches. Mini Bundtlette pans (4 x 2 inches) are also available and make ideal individual desserts. Tube pans are commonly found in 9 x 4 inch or 10 x 4 inch sizes. Some tube pans have feet that make them ideal to invert foam-style cakes for cooling.

**PARCHMENT PAPER:** Lining loaf and layer pans with parchment prevents the cake from sticking to the pan and produces straighter bottoms and cake sides. It also makes cleaning up easier. Cut parchment into circles to fit the appropriate size pan (e.g., 8- or 9-inch round). Then cut parchment into 2-inch-wide strips. I usually cut a bunch of strips in various sizes just to have them handy. Spray the cake pans with non-stick spray, then line the bottom of the pan with the circle of parchment. Use the strips to adhere to the sides of the pan. This also eliminates the messy task of greasing and flouring pans.

When using a tube pan for butter-based cakes, you can cut the parchment to adhere around the inner tube. When spraying, try to hold the pan and spray over the sink. This helps to eliminate messy overspray. If you're using foil loaf pans and are giving them as gifts, in the pan, you don't need to line the pan with parchment. Just grease and flour, or spray with nonstick spray.

For fluted Bundt pans that can't be lined with parchment, carefully grease with vegetable shortening, being sure you grease every crevice. Dust with flour to coat pan. This will prevent the cake from sticking. Spread shortening over inside of pans using your fingers or a pastry brush.

When baking chocolate cakes, dust the greased pan with cocoa instead of flour to avoid any white blotches on the cake. If you absolutely hate to grease and flour, you can use a nonstick cooking spray. I've found this method to have irregular results, whereas the traditional method of greasing and flouring is virtually foolproof.

**MIXING BOWLS AND UTENSILS:** You will need the usual types of mixing bowls, rubber spatulas, cake testers, measuring cups, and spoons that are normally found in most kitchens.

**ELECTRIC MIXERS:** Hand-held electric mixers will work fine, but a stand-up mixer is a great tool to have. This allows you to walk away from the mixer while butter is creaming, for example, and do another task like prepare cake pans.

You'll need a hand-held mixer to make our Seven-Minute Frosting. This frosting is mixed in a double boiler over boiling water, so it would be impossible to use a stand-up mixer.

**DOUBLE BOILERS:** These are pots that fit together, with one pot in another. The lower pot holds water that either simmers or boils to gently cook whatever is in the upper pot. If you don't have a double boiler, you can carefully use a saucepan filled with water as the bottom, and a stainless steel bowl that fits over the top.

**WIRE COOLING RACKS:** These are necessary to cool cakes properly. They allow air to circulate around and underneath the cake to cool it completely. Wire racks are also great while glazing the top of a cake with confectioners' frosting. Place a piece of parchment or waxed paper under the wire rack to catch any excess frosting that drips off.

**OVENS:** The recipes in this book are timed using a moderate oven, either gas or electric. If you are using a convection oven, your baking times will be less than the recommended times. Please consult your owner's manual for more specific baking times.

I don't suggest going out and purchasing a new oven, but oven doors with windows and ovens with lights are ideal for anxious cake bakers. This allows you to glimpse the progress of baking without actually opening the oven and disturbing the baking process. You can cause the cake to fall if you open the oven door too soon and let cold air in.

Be sure to check your oven temperature. Many bakers assume their ovens work fine because they cook roasts and casseroles well. Remember that cakes are sensitive and need the proper heat to generate volume. Use an oven thermometer to check for accurate temperatures. These are inexpensive and can give you an accurate reading. If the oven temperature is too low or high, call a repairman to make the proper adjustments.

## GENERAL INFORMATION AND TECHNIQUES

### Room-Temperature Ingredients

I stress once again that all the cake ingredients should be at room temperature. This is the only way to ensure that all of the elements will blend together successfully and smoothly. A good way to start is to read through the recipe first so that you understand all the directions. Then organize your ingredients according to mixing order to be sure you don't forget anything. Also, prepare your pans before you begin mixing so that you can get the cakes in the oven as soon as they're mixed.

## Mixing Methods

There are several methods for blending ingredients together. One is the creaming method. This is commonly used for butter cakes. The butter or shortening is creamed first, then the sugar is gradually added and blended until light. Eggs are added one at a time. It's important to the volume and structure of the cake that one egg is well incorporated before adding the next egg. After the eggs and extracts are added, the dry ingredients are added. Usually all the dry ingredients (flour, baking powder, salt, etc.) are combined together. They are either added slowly or added alternately with some type of liquid (such as milk, buttermilk, or sour cream). It's important not to overmix at this point. If overbeaten, the cake can become dry and tough. Blend just until smooth and pour into the prepared pan.

## Foam Cake Mixing

This technique is used primarily with angel food and sponge-type cakes. With sponge cakes, the egg whites and yolks are separated. The yolks are beaten with sugar until thick and uniformly yellow. In another bowl, the whites are whipped until stiff but not dry. Flour is added to the yolk mixture. The yolks are then carefully folded into the egg white mixture using a rubber spatula. The batter is poured into an ungreased pan. The angel food technique is the same as above, without the yolk stage.

## How to Fold in Beaten Egg Whites

It's important to have a light hand while folding. Using a rubber spatula, with small wrist turning strokes, add air as you incorporate ingredients. Be sure to scrape the bottom of the bowl with your turning strokes.

## How to Tell When a Cake Is Done

The traditional method of checking for doneness is to stick a cake tester into the center of the cake. When the tester comes out clean, the cake is done. Sometimes, however, when a tester comes out clean, the cake ends up overdone because it will continue cooking in the pan. I've found it best to remove a cake when the tester comes out with a small crumb. Not batter, just a fine crumb.

## Cooling Cakes

Most butter-based cakes should be cooled in the pan, on wire cooling racks, after removal from the oven. Most cakes at this point are too fragile to be turned out of the pans; they will break. After cooling in the pan for 5 to 10 minutes, remove cake from the hot pan, carefully flipping the cake bottom side down on the wire cooling rack. If you leave the cake top side down on the cooling rack, it can split. You can easily flip the cake bottom side down by using another wire rack to turn it.

Continue cooling for 15 to 20 minutes on cooling rack. If you are going to frost the cake, leave it on the rack until fully cool. Otherwise, when almost cool, wrap in foil, then plastic. Store at room temperature overnight or freeze for later use.

Angel food and sponge cakes are baked in tube pans. They need to be inverted for proper cooling. Many older models of tube pans will have feet extending from the top of the pan. If you have a pan with feet, simply turn it upside down and let the cake stand on a clean counter or table until cool. If your tube pan does not have feet, you can invert the pan onto the neck of a soda bottle. Although it may look precarious, this method will hold the cake firmly on top of the bottle and it will hang there and cool successfully. To remove sponge cakes from the pan, use a long, sharp knife. Run the knife around the sides of the tube pan. Loosen the inside cone. Run the knife around the inside cone and underneath the bottom of the cake.

## Frosting

Frost cakes only when completely cool. There will be less breakage and crumbs if the cake is frosted the day after baking. If unfrosted cake layers have been frozen, thaw them first, then frost.

## Dusting with Confectioners' Sugar

To dust a cake or cake slice with confectioners' sugar, place a few tablespoons of powdered sugar in a small dry strainer. Hold the strainer over the cake and with a teaspoon stir the sugar over the cake in the desired amount.

## Storage

Wrap unfrosted cake in foil, then plastic. Freeze up to two months. Thaw cake in the refrigerator before serving or frosting.

Store cakes frosted with a buttercream icing in the refrigerator for two to three days. Once a cake has been frosted with a buttercream frosting, it is sealed. Bring to room temperature before serving.

Cakes frosted with whipped cream can stay refrigerated for one to two days. Whipped cream is a more porous frosting, so it doesn't have the sealing capabilities of buttercream. Keep whipped cream cakes away from odors in the refrigerator. The cream will absorb odors.

## Shipping

Unfrosted loaf and Bundt cakes can be shipped through the mail, but layer cakes with frosting are not recommended for shipping. If you need to ship a cake, be sure to use a heavy corrugated cardboard shipping box. Wrap the cake in plastic to secure freshness, and perhaps use a cookie tin or wrap with some cellophane and ribbon. Be sure to properly cushion the cake with newspaper or tissue paper. Use the quickest service possible to ship perishable food items.

## Determining Serving Quantities

Many of these recipes for layer cakes are for either 8- or 9-inch cakes. These cakes serve 10 to 12, and 12 to 15 respectively. If you're having a larger party, I recommend making two different types of cakes—perhaps one chocolate and one another flavor.

The number of servings will vary with loaf and tube pans. Although they are standard-size pans, the type of cake will dictate the number of servings. A dense fruit-filled butter cake should be cut into thin pieces. Because these types of cakes are rich, they will yield more servings than a light, plain angel food cake.

## Baking for Company

When baking or cooking for guests, it is less stressful to prepare a recipe that you've already tried. This way you know if you like the cake and what to expect for preparation time. It's also a good idea to prepare as many elements ahead of time as possible. For example, if you are having a party on a Saturday night, bake your cake and make your filling on Friday. Make your frosting and assemble the cake on Saturday morning.

## How to Whip Cream

If you're whipping the cream to use as a dollop on a slice of cake, you don't need to beat until very stiff. Stiff whipped cream is necessary only if you're filling and frosting a layer cake.

Chill the mixing bowl and beaters for 10 to 15 minutes before whipping cream. Use a fresh heavy cream. Whip with an electric mixer using wire whisk attachment. Whip at high speed until medium peaks form, about 2 minutes. Add granulated sugar and continue whipping another 30 seconds, or until stiff. Use immediately.

### BASIC CAKE DECORATING TIPS AND EQUIPMENT

Here are a few basic items that are great for decorating cakes.

## Pastry Bags and Tips

Don't be intimidated by a pastry bag. It's a great tool to use to assemble and decorate layer cakes. If you're just starting to use a pastry bag, I recommend using the flexible plastic reusable type. These are pliable, easy to use, and easy to clean. Some of the older cloth pastry bags absorb greasy frostings, are hard to dry, and can become stiff with age. The only decorating tip you may need for the cakes in this book is the basic star tip, usually numbered 32 by most manufacturers. We won't spend a lot of time on decorating techniques—just enough to assemble your layer cake and perhaps make a simple shell border.

### Spatulas and Combs

Straight metal spatulas are recommended for frosting cakes. Try to find the length that you are most comfortable with. I prefer a wooden-handled 6 x 3-inch version. Metal scrapers, found in most kitchen shops, are another great tool to help you smooth the sides of your layer cakes. You can also purchase, quite inexpensively, a triangular cake comb that will give your sides a ribbed effect. Just hold the comb against the sides of your cake as you turn the cake on your turntable.

### Turntables

Professional cake decorators use a turntable to spin cakes around for easier decorating. You can use the same technique at home by using a lazy susan to turn your cake as you frost it.

### Cake Bases

A flat, sturdy plate can serve as the base for your decorated cake. If you are bringing the cake somewhere and don't want to worry about getting your plate back, use a cardboard cake circle. These corrugated cardboard circles can be purchased at specialty kitchen or party shops. Use a cardboard base that is at least two inches larger than your cake. For exceptionally heavy or large cakes, double or triple the cardboard thickness.

A nice way to present your cake is to use a doily on top of your cake base. Use a bit of buttercream to adhere the doily to the cake base and to adhere the cake to the doily to prevent any slipping of your cake.

To keep your doily clean as you decorate, place a piece of cellophane or plastic wrap over the entire doily surface. Then place the bottom cake layer on the plastic or cellophane. After decorating, carefully cut away the excess plastic, leaving the clean doily.

### Frosting

The easiest way to frost a layer cake is to start from the top. Pile some frosting on top of your filled layer cake. Working from the center, spread the frosting to the edges with your metal spatula. Work the frosting onto the sides of the cake, covering all areas. It's always best to pile on more frosting. Be generous. After you get the frosting on, you can eliminate the excess with your spatula, metal scraper, or comb. If you're working with a dense frosting like a buttercream, it's a good idea to have a bowl of hot water nearby. You can dip your spatula, scraper, and/or comb into the water to help spread the frosting and help to release it from the spatula.

For fancy smooth finishes with buttercream icings, it's best to apply two coats of frosting. The first coat is called the crumb coat. This is a thin layer that you apply without worrying about crumbs in the frosting. Refrigerate the crumb-coated cake for about 30 minutes, or until hard to the touch. Now you can apply the crumb-free finish coat of frosting to the cake.

Whipped cream frostings are easier to spread than buttercream frostings and require only one coat. It is important that you use the whipped cream immediately after whipping it. Frost quickly to be sure that the frosting stays firm.

## Filling a Pastry Bag

An easy way to fill a pastry bag is to place the tip side down in a tall drinking glass. Fold the top edges of the bag down around the outside of the glass. Spoon your frosting into the open bag, being careful not to overfill it. Gather up the top edges and remove from the glass. To use, simply squeeze and add pressure to the center of the bag. This will release the frosting through the tip.

## Making a Dam

For many loose fillings such as custards and lemon curd, you will need to make a frosting dam to hold the filling in. Using a pastry bag fitted with a basic star tip (or no tip at all), simply pipe a line of frosting around the perimeter of the layer of cake. Spoon your filling inside the frosting outline and place the top layer of cake on top.

## Piping a Shell Border

A shell border is a basic border for the top and bottom of a layer cake, made with a pastry bag and, most often, an open star tip (#32). Practice on a flat surface, such as a parchment-lined cookie sheet. You can then scrape up frosting, refill the pastry bag, and practice again. You can use a top and bottom border to frame your cakes or just a top border.

## Covering Your Mistakes

One of the easiest things to do when decorating is to cover your mistakes. With many of the cakes in this book, you don't have to be fussy about frosting the cake sides and tops. While the frosting is still wet, cover the frosting with chopped nuts, coconut, or colored sprinkles. This is an easy way to get a professional look without the headaches of professional cake decorating. Garnish generously with sliced fruit or chocolate pieces, candy, or fresh, nonpoisonous, unsprayed flowers and herbs. These are simple elegant ways to garnish a cake. Remember that your cake doesn't need to have a structured, store-bought look. A natural, simple home-baked look is more appetizing and shows that you've spent the time and energy to produce something of your own.

### Other Enhancements

If you don't want to decorate your cake, decorate around it. Pretty platters, doilies, candles, tablecloths, and floral arrangements can all enhance the presentation of your desserts.

# LOAF AND BUNDT CAKES

## LOAF AND BUNDT CAKE TIPS

*Loaf and Bundt cakes are a great place to start cake baking. These are simple cakes that can be garnished and glazed to make a perfect dessert or a perfect brunch accompaniment. The loaf cakes in this collection include fine-textured butter cakes, fruitcakes, and coffee cakes. A lot of these cakes have long cooking times because of their height. But you can put the cake in the oven and almost forget about it while you do something else.*

*Try to follow the recipe for pan-size requirements, otherwise your baking times and servings will be different. These recipes are flexible so that if you want to use two loaf pans instead of one Bundt pan, you can. Just be sure to adjust your baking time. Two smaller loaf pans will bake quicker than one Bundt pan. These types of cakes freeze best without any dusting or frosting. Simply wrap in foil, then plastic, and freeze. Thaw, frost, and enjoy.*

# BASIC POUND CAKE

*This is a classic and should be a part of every baker's repertoire. It offers great flexibility; you can pair it with almost any frosting or garnish. The name "pound cake" comes from the original measurements used to make this cake: one pound of butter, one pound of sugar, one pound of eggs, and one pound of flour.*

| | |
|---|---|
| ½ POUND BUTTER, SOFTENED | 2 CUPS CAKE FLOUR |
| 1½ CUPS SUGAR | 1 TEASPOON BAKING POWDER |
| 1 TEASPOON VANILLA EXTRACT | PINCH OF SALT |
| 4 EGGS | CONFECTIONERS' SUGAR FOR DUSTING |

1.  Preheat oven to 350°F.

2.  Grease and flour or line a 10 x 6 x 2½-inch loaf pan with parchment paper. Set aside.

3.  In an electric mixer, cream butter on medium speed. Gradually add sugar and beat until light in color.

4.  Add vanilla. Scrape down the sides of the mixing bowl to be sure mixture is well blended. Add eggs, one at a time, beating well after each egg.

5.  On low speed, blend in flour, baking powder, and salt just until blended.

6.  Pour batter into prepared pan. Bake for 50 to 55 minutes, or until a tester comes out with a fine crumb.

7.  Remove pan from the oven and place on wire cooling rack. Let cool in pan for 10 minutes. Carefully remove cake from the pan and continue to cool on wire rack until cool. Remove and discard parchment.

8.  Dust the top with confectioners' sugar and serve. Store unused cake wrapped in plastic wrap at room temperature or freeze for later use.

YIELD: ONE LARGE LOAF, ABOUT 12 SLICES

# ALMOND POUND CAKE

*This family recipe is a popular variation of the Basic Pound Cake, accented by a rich burst of almond. My dad loves this cake topped with Strawberries in Vermouth (page 59) and a dollop of whipped cream.*

| | |
|---|---|
| 12 TABLESPOONS BUTTER, SOFTENED | 2 CUPS CAKE FLOUR |
| ¾ CUP ALMOND PASTE | 2 TEASPOONS BAKING POWDER |
| 1 CUP SUGAR | 1 TEASPOON SALT |
| 4 EGGS | ¾ CUP MILK |
| 1 TEASPOON VANILLA EXTRACT | |

1. Preheat oven to 350°F.

2. Grease and flour or line a 10 x 6 x 2½-inch loaf pan with parchment paper. Set aside.

3. In an electric mixer on medium speed, cream the butter. Add almond paste and mix until smooth. Gradually add sugar and beat until light in color.

4. Add eggs, one at a time, mixing well after each egg. Add vanilla.

5. In a small bowl, combine flour, baking powder, and salt. Add this mixture alternately with the milk, beginning and ending with the flour mixture. Mix just until blended.

6. Pour batter into prepared pan. Bake for 55 to 60 minutes, or until a tester comes out with a fine crumb.

7. Remove cake from the oven and cool in pan on wire cooling rack for 10 to 15 minutes.

8. Carefully remove cake from the pan and continue to cool on wire cooling rack. When cool, serve or wrap in foil. Store at room temperature or wrap in foil and plastic, then freeze.

This cake can also be used for the Frozen Almond Strawberry Cake (page 103).

YIELD: ONE LARGE LOAF, ABOUT 12 SLICES

# PUMPKIN RAISIN CAKE

*This is a moist and spicy autumn favorite that's not too sweet. It's ideal served plain, alongside a savory soup, or topped with Cream Cheese Frosting (page 122) for a true New England dessert.*

| | |
|---|---|
| 3 EGGS | 1½ TEASPOONS BAKING POWDER |
| 1¼ CUPS SUGAR | 1½ TEASPOONS CINNAMON |
| 1½ CUPS CANNED PUMPKIN | 1 TEASPOON SALT |
| 1¼ CUPS VEGETABLE OIL | 1 TEASPOON BAKING SODA |
| 1½ CUPS UNBLEACHED FLOUR | 1¼ CUPS RAISINS |

1. Preheat oven to 350°F.

2. Grease and flour or line a 10 x 6 x 2½-inch loaf pan with parchment paper.

3. In an electric mixer, mix eggs, sugar, pumpkin, and oil on medium speed until well blended, 2 to 3 minutes.

4. On low speed, gradually add flour, baking powder, cinnamon, salt, and baking soda. Mix just until smooth. Stir in raisins.

5. Pour batter evenly into prepared pan.

6. Bake for 45 to 50 minutes, or until a tester comes out with a fine crumb. Remove pan from the oven and place on wire cooling rack. Cool cake in pan for 10 to 15 minutes.

7. Carefully remove cake from the pan and place on wire cooling rack. Remove and discard parchment.

8. Store at room temperature, wrapped in foil or a plastic bag. Or freeze for later use.

YIELD: ONE LARGE LOAF, ABOUT 12 SLICES

# DOT'S ZUCCHINI WALNUT CAKE

*This favorite breakfast cake was made by a friend's mom who always baked a batch to take along on family trips. She'd bake one with nuts and one without, to suit everyone in her family. Try a lightly toasted slice with butter or cream cheese.*

3 EGGS

1 CUP VEGETABLE OIL

2 CUPS SUGAR

2 TEASPOONS VANILLA EXTRACT

3 CUPS FINELY CHOPPED OR GRATED ZUCCHINI

2 CUPS ALL-PURPOSE FLOUR

¼ TEASPOON BAKING POWDER

1 TEASPOON BAKING SODA

2 TEASPOONS CINNAMON

¼ TEASPOON SALT

1 CUP WALNUTS, COARSELY CHOPPED

1. Preheat oven to 350°F.

2. Grease and flour or line a 10 x 6 x 2½-inch loaf pan with parchment paper. Set aside.

3. In an electric mixer on medium speed, beat eggs. Add oil, sugar, and vanilla and beat until light. Add zucchini.

4. On low speed, gradually add flour, baking powder, baking soda, cinnamon, and salt. Mix just until blended. Stir in walnuts.

5. Pour batter into prepared pan.

6. Bake for 1 hour and 15 to 20 minutes, or until a tester comes out with a fine crumb.

7. Remove pan from the oven. Cool in pan on a wire cooling rack for 10 to 15 minutes. Carefully remove cake from the pan and continue to cool on wire rack. Remove and discard parchment.

YIELD: ONE LARGE LOAF, ABOUT 12 SLICES

# RUSTIC APPLE CAKE

*This apple and cinnamon cake is a hearty dessert for any occasion. It's great served slightly warm with a scoop of vanilla ice cream. Be sure to line the tube pan with parchment. The apples can get a little sticky without it.*

1½ CUPS PLUS 2 TABLESPOONS SUGAR

2 TEASPOONS CINNAMON

1 CUP CHOPPED WALNUTS, OPTIONAL

6 EGGS

½ CUP VEGETABLE OIL

4 TABLESPOONS LEMON JUICE

GRATED RIND OF 1 LEMON

1 TEASPOON VANILLA EXTRACT

2 CUPS ALL-PURPOSE FLOUR

2 TEASPOONS BAKING POWDER

4 APPLES, CORED, PEELED, AND THINLY SLICED (ABOUT 4 CUPS)

1. Preheat oven to 350°F.

2. Grease and flour or line a 10-inch tube pan with parchment paper. Set aside.

3. In a small bowl, combine 2 tablespoons sugar, cinnamon, and walnuts. Set aside.

4. In an electric mixer on medium speed, mix eggs, 1½ cups sugar, oil, lemon juice, lemon rind, and vanilla. On low speed, add flour and baking powder. Mix until batter is smooth.

5. Pour half the batter into prepared pan. Spread half the apple slices over batter. Sprinkle with half the cinnamon and sugar mixture. Pour remaining batter over apples. Spread the remaining apple slices on top and sprinkle with remaining cinnamon and sugar.

6. Bake for 60 to 65 minutes, or until a tester comes out with a fine crumb. Remove pan from the oven and cool in pan on wire cooling rack. Be sure that this cake is very cool before you remove it from the pan.

YIELD: ONE 10-INCH CAKE, ABOUT 25 SLICES

# CITRUS YOGURT CAKE

*This light and zesty cake is ideal for summer picnics and parties. This is my favorite*
*version, using a combination of lemons and limes. You can use either one*
*or the other, or try using oranges.*

| | |
|---|---|
| ½ POUND BUTTER, SOFTENED | 1 CUP PLAIN YOGURT |
| 2 CUPS SUGAR | 2¼ CUPS CAKE FLOUR |
| 3 EGGS | ½ TEASPOON BAKING SODA |
| GRATED RIND OF 2 LEMONS | ¼ TEASPOON SALT |
| GRATED RIND OF 2 LIMES | JUICE OF 2 LIMES |
| JUICE OF 2 LEMONS | CONFECTIONERS' SUGAR FOR DUSTING |

1. Preheat oven to 350°F.

2. Grease and flour or line two 8 x 4 x 3-inch loaf pans with parchment paper. Set aside.

3. In an electric mixer on medium speed, cream butter. Add sugar gradually and beat until light in color.

4. Add eggs, one at a time, beating well after adding each one. Add lemon and lime rind and lemon juice. Add yogurt and blend well.

5. On low speed, add flour, baking soda, and salt. Mix just until blended. Pour batter into prepared pans. Spread batter evenly in pans.

6. Bake for 55 to 60 minutes, or until a tester comes out with a fine crumb.

7. Remove from the oven. Pour lime juice over the hot cakes. Cool cakes in pans for 20 to 25 minutes. Carefully remove cakes from the pans and continue to cool on wire cooling racks. Cool completely. Remove and discard parchment.

8. Dust with confectioners' sugar or Confectioners' Glaze (page 54) and serve.

YIELD: TWO SMALL LOAVES, ABOUT 12 SLICES EACH

# BLUEBERRY BANANA CAKE

*This tasty breakfast cake uses mashed bananas for the perfect complement to fresh blueberries. Try a slice with your morning coffee or a hot herbal tea. If fresh blueberries are not available, frozen ones will work just as well.*

¼ POUND BUTTER, SOFTENED

2 CUPS PLUS 1 TABLESPOON SUGAR

3 EGGS

½ CUP MASHED BANANAS (1½ MEDIUM BANANAS)

3 CUPS PLUS 1 TABLESPOON ALL-PURPOSE FLOUR

PINCH OF SALT

1½ TEASPOONS BAKING POWDER

½ CUP MILK

2 CUPS FRESH OR FROZEN BLUEBERRIES

1. Preheat oven to 350°F.

2. Grease and flour a 9-inch fluted Bundt pan. Set aside.

3. In an electric mixer on medium speed, cream the butter. Gradually add sugar. Add eggs, one at a time, beating well after each one. Add mashed bananas.

4. In a separate bowl, mix flour, salt, and baking powder. Add flour mixture to the butter mixture alternately with the milk, starting and ending with the flour mixture. Mix until just blended and smooth.

5. In a separate bowl, mix blueberries with 1 tablespoon flour and 1 tablespoon sugar to coat. Stir coated blueberries into batter. Pour into prepared pan.

6. Bake for 60 to 65 minutes, or until a tester comes out with a fine crumb. Remove cake from oven and place on wire cooling rack. Cool cake in pan for 15 to 20 minutes. Remove cake from pan and continue to cool, right side up, on cooling rack.

YIELD: ONE 9-INCH CAKE, ABOUT 20 SLICES

# APRICOT NUT CAKE

*This dense butter cake accented with dried apricots updates a classic family fruitcake recipe. For this cake, and most fruitcakes, coat the fruit and nuts with flour before adding to your batter. This will keep them from sinking to the bottom of the cake.*

1½ CUPS PECANS, COARSELY CHOPPED

1½ CUPS DRIED APRICOTS, COARSELY CHOPPED

3½ CUPS CAKE FLOUR

½ POUND BUTTER, SOFTENED

2 CUPS SUGAR

2 TEASPOONS VANILLA EXTRACT

4 EGGS

1 TEASPOON BAKING SODA

1½ CUPS SOUR CREAM

CONFECTIONERS' SUGAR FOR DUSTING

GLAZE:

¼ CUP RUM

½ CUP ORANGE JUICE

1. Preheat oven to 350°F.

2. Grease and flour or line two 10 x 6 x 2½-inch loaf pans with parchment paper. Set aside.

3. Combine nuts and apricots in a small bowl. Toss them with 3 tablespoons of the flour. Coat well. Set aside.

4. In an electric mixer on medium speed, cream butter and sugar until light in color. Add vanilla. Add eggs, one at a time, mixing well after each egg. Scrape down the sides of the bowl.

5. Combine flour and baking soda. Add flour mixture to the butter mixture, gradually at low speed, alternating with the sour cream. Start and end with the flour mixture. Mix just until blended.

6. Stir in nuts and apricots. Spoon batter equally into prepared loaf pans.

7. Bake for 50 to 55 minutes, or until a tester comes out with a fine crumb. Remove pans from the oven. Place on wire cooling racks.

8. In a small cup, mix together rum and orange juice. Pour evenly over the hot cakes. Cool cakes in pans for 15 to 20 minutes. Remove cakes from the pans and

continue cooling the cakes on wire racks until cool. Remove and discard parchment. Dust with confectioners' sugar before serving, or freeze.

YIELD: TWO LARGE LOAVES, ABOUT 12 SLICES EACH

---

◆ **DECORATING AND SERVING LOAF AND** ◆
**BUNDT CAKES**

THROUGHOUT THE BOOK I'VE MADE SERVING SUGGESTIONS, PAIRING CAKES WITH GARNISHES. THESE ARE MERELY SUGGESTIONS. FEEL FREE TO MAKE UP YOUR OWN COMBINATIONS. YOU CAN ALSO SIMPLY DUST THE TOP WITH CONFECTIONERS' SUGAR, USE A GLAZE DRIZZLED OVER THE TOP, OR TOP A SLICE OF CAKE WITH A SCOOP OF ICE CREAM OR WHIPPED CREAM AND FRESH FRUIT.

A NICE SIMPLE WAY TO SERVE A PIECE OF CAKE IS TO SPREAD A FRUIT SAUCE ON THE PLATE, TOP WITH A SLICE OF CAKE, AND ADD ANOTHER DRIZZLE OF SAUCE ON TOP. DRIZZLE BY DIPPING A FORK INTO A FRUIT OR FUDGE SAUCE, THEN SHAKE THE SAUCE ONTO THE CAKE.

---

# CRANBERRY NUT BUNDT CAKE

*Cranberries, dates, and walnuts make the perfect combination for holiday gatherings. This is the first of many recipes given to me by my mother-in-law. She easily doubles this recipe and makes extra cakes that are ideal holiday gifts for teachers or neighbors.*

2 EGGS

1 CUP SUGAR

¾ CUP VEGETABLE OIL

2½ CUPS ALL-PURPOSE FLOUR

1 TEASPOON BAKING POWDER

1 TEASPOON BAKING SODA

1 CUP BUTTERMILK

1 CUP WHOLE CRANBERRIES, FRESH OR FROZEN

1 CUP CHOPPED DATES

1 CUP WALNUTS, COARSELY CHOPPED

CONFECTIONERS' SUGAR FOR DUSTING

GLAZE:

¼ CUP ORANGE JUICE

¼ CUP WHISKEY

1. Preheat oven to 350°F.

2. Grease and flour a 9-inch Bundt pan. Set aside.

3. In an electric mixer on medium speed, mix eggs, sugar, and oil. In a separate bowl, blend flour, baking powder, and baking soda. Gradually add the flour mixture, alternately with the buttermilk, on low speed. Start and end with the flour mixture. Mix just until blended.

4. Fold in cranberries, dates, and walnuts. Pour batter into prepared pan. Bake for 25 to 30 minutes, or until a tester comes out with a fine crumb. Remove cake from the oven and place on wire cooling rack. Mix orange juice and whiskey and pour over hot cake.

5. Cool cake in pan for 10 to 15 minutes. Carefully remove cake from the pan and continue cooling on wire cooling rack. Dust with confectioners' sugar or frost with Confectioners' Glaze (page 54).

YIELD: ONE 9-INCH CAKE, ABOUT 20 SLICES

# PECAN DATE BOURBON CAKE

*This nut-and-date-studded cake has a subtle orange flavor. The bourbon orange juice glaze keeps it fresh and moist for days. It's an ideal cake to bake and give for that perfect thank you.*

| | |
|---|---|
| 12 TABLESPOONS BUTTER, SOFTENED | ½ TEASPOON SALT |
| 1½ CUPS SUGAR | 1½ TEASPOONS BAKING SODA |
| 1 TEASPOON VANILLA EXTRACT | 1½ CUPS BUTTERMILK |
| 1 TABLESPOON GRATED ORANGE RIND | 1 CUP PECANS, COARSELY CHOPPED |
| 3 EGGS | 1 CUP DATES, CHOPPED |
| 3 CUPS CAKE FLOUR | CONFECTIONERS' SUGAR FOR DUSTING |

**GLAZE:**

| | |
|---|---|
| ¼ CUP ORANGE JUICE | 2 TABLESPOONS BOURBON |

1. Preheat oven to 350°F.

2. Grease and flour a 9-inch Bundt pan. Set aside.

3. In an electric mixer on medium speeed, cream the butter. Gradually add sugar and beat until light in color. Add vanilla and orange rind. Beat until blended. Add eggs, one at a time, beating well after adding each one.

4. Combine flour, salt, and baking soda in a separate bowl. Add flour mixture to the butter mixture alternately with the buttermilk. Begin and end with the flour mixture. Mix until smooth. Stir in pecans and dates. Pour batter into prepared pan.

5. Bake for 40 to 45 minutes, or until a tester comes out with a fine crumb. Remove cake from the oven. Cool cake in pan on wire rack. While cake is hot, mix orange juice and bourbon and pour over the cake. Cool in pan for 10 to 15 minutes. Remove cake from the pan. Continue to cool on wire rack until cool.

6. Dust top with confectioners' sugar and serve.

YIELD: ONE 9-INCH CAKE, ABOUT 20 SLICES

# COCONUT POUND CAKE

*This moist and sweet cake is great served plain or topped with a spoonful of crushed pineapple and a dollop of whipped cream for a piña colada dessert.*

| | |
|---|---|
| ½ POUND UNSALTED BUTTER | 1 TEASPOON BAKING POWDER |
| 2 CUPS SUGAR | ¼ TEASPOON SALT |
| 1 TEASPOON VANILLA EXTRACT | 1 CUP MILK |
| 4 EGGS | 1½ CUPS SHREDDED COCONUT |
| 2½ CUPS CAKE FLOUR | |

1. Preheat oven to 350°F.

2. Grease and flour or line two 8 x 4 x 3-inch loaf pans with parchment paper. Set aside.

3. In an electric mixer on medium speed, cream the butter. Gradually add the sugar and beat until light in color. Add vanilla. Add eggs, one at a time, beating well after each egg.

4. In a small bowl, combine flour, baking powder, and salt. On low speed, add to the butter mixture alternately with the milk. Start and end with the flour mixture. Mix just until blended. Stir in coconut. Pour batter into prepared pans.

5. Bake for 55 to 60 minutes, or until a tester comes out with a fine crumb. Remove cakes from the oven and cool on wire cooling racks for 10 to 15 minutes. If you're using foil pans, continue cooling the cakes completely in the pans. If you're using a traditional cake pan, carefully remove the cakes from the pan and continue to cool on wire cooling racks until completely cool.

YIELD: TWO LOAVES, ABOUT 12 SLICES EACH

# HOLIDAY FRUITCAKE

*This recipe is one of my mom's holiday specialties. Use a combination of red and green cherries for a festive Christmas look. Save a slice for Santa.*

| | |
|---|---|
| 8 OUNCES CREAM CHEESE, SOFTENED | 1½ TEASPOONS BAKING POWDER |
| ½ POUND BUTTER | 2 CUPS GLACÉ CHERRY HALVES |
| 1½ CUPS SUGAR | 2 CUPS WALNUTS, COARSELY CHOPPED |
| 1 TEASPOON VANILLA EXTRACT | ½ CUP CHOPPED DATES |
| 4 EGGS | ½ CUP RAISINS |
| 2 CUPS PLUS 3 TABLESPOONS ALL-PURPOSE FLOUR | ¼ CUP WHISKEY |
| | CONFECTIONERS' SUGAR FOR DUSTING |

1. Preheat oven to 325°F.

2. Grease and flour a 9-inch Bundt pan. Set aside.

3. In an electric mixer on medium speed, cream the cream cheese until fluffy, about 3 minutes. Add butter. Beat until smooth. Gradually add sugar and beat until light.

4. Add vanilla. Add eggs, one at a time, beating well after each one. On low speed, gradually add 2 cups flour and baking powder. Mix just until blended.

5. In a medium mixing bowl, combine cherries, nuts, dates, and raisins. Toss with 3 tablespoons of flour to coat. Fold fruit and nut mixture into batter. Pour batter into prepared pan.

6. Bake for 55 to 60 minutes, or until a tester comes out with a fine crumb. Remove pan from the oven and place on a wire cooling rack. Pour whiskey evenly over the hot cake. Cool cake in pan for 10 to 15 minutes. Carefully remove from pan and continue to cool on wire cooling rack. Store at room temperature wrapped in foil, or freeze. Dust with confectioners' sugar or frost with Confectioners' Glaze (page 54) before serving.

YIELD: ONE 9-INCH CAKE, ABOUT 25 SLICES

# CARIBBEAN FRUITCAKE

*This dark, rich fruitcake is full of flavor from rum-soaked fruit. This type of fruitcake originated in the islands, where spices, molasses, and rum were plentiful.*

2 CUPS RAISINS

1 CUP DATES, CHOPPED

1 CAN CRUSHED PINEAPPLE, WITH JUICE

1 CUP SLICED ALMONDS

1 CUP CURRANTS

½ CUP DARK RUM

½ POUND BUTTER, SOFTENED

2 CUPS DARK BROWN SUGAR

5 EGGS

2 CUPS ALL-PURPOSE FLOUR

2 TEASPOONS BAKING POWDER

1 ½ TEASPOONS ALLSPICE

PINCH OF SALT

CONFECTIONERS' SUGAR FOR DUSTING

1. In a medium mixing bowl combine raisins, dates, pineapple, almonds, currants, and rum. Let soak for 1 to 2 hours at room temperature.

2. Preheat oven to 350°F.

3. Grease and flour or line a 10-inch tube pan with parchment paper. Set aside.

4. In an electric mixer on medium speed, cream the butter. Gradually add the brown sugar and beat until light in color. Add eggs, one at a time, beating well after each egg.

5. On low speed, gradually add the flour, baking powder, allspice, and salt. Mix just until blended. Fold in fruit mixture. Pour batter into prepared pan.

6. Bake for 60 to 65 minutes, or until a tester comes out with a fine crumb. Remove cake from the oven and place on wire cooling rack. Cool cake in pan for 20 to 25 minutes. Carefully remove cake from the pan and continue to cool on wire rack. Store at room temperature wrapped in foil, or freeze. Dust with confectioners' sugar before serving.

YIELD: ONE 10-INCH CAKE, ABOUT 30 SLICES

# CHOCOLATE MAYONNAISE CAKE

*This cake combines one of my least favorite things, mayonnaise, with one of my favorite things, chocolate. It may sound like an odd match, but since mayonnaise is basically eggs and oil, it's the perfect secret ingredient for making this light, moist cake. It works with a number of toppings. Try it with a spoonful of Raspberry Sauce (page 58), ice cream, and fresh berries.*

| | |
|---|---|
| 2 CUPS CAKE FLOUR | ¼ TEASPOON SALT |
| 1½ CUPS SUGAR | 1 CUP COLD BREWED COFFEE |
| 2 TEASPOONS BAKING SODA | 1 CUP MAYONNAISE |
| ½ CUP COCOA | 1 TEASPOON VANILLA EXTRACT |

1. Preheat oven to 350°F.

2. Grease and flour or line a 10 x 6 x 2½-inch loaf pan with parchment paper. Set aside.

3. In an electric mixer on low speed, blend flour, sugar, baking soda, cocoa, and salt. Add coffee, mayonnaise, and vanilla. Beat until smooth and well blended, about 2 minutes.

4. Pour batter into prepared pan. Bake for 25 to 30 minutes, or until a tester comes out with a fine crumb. Remove cake from the oven and cool in pan on wire cooling rack for 10 to 15 minutes.

5. Carefully remove cake from the pan and continue to cool top side up on wire cooling rack. Remove and discard parchment.

6. Serve, or wrap in foil and store at room temperature, or freeze.

YIELD: ONE LARGE LOAF, ABOUT 12 SLICES

# NEW ENGLAND MAPLE
# WALNUT CAKE

*Top this cake with a dollop of whipped cream or a scoop of ice cream and a drizzle of maple syrup. It's the perfect way to conclude an autumn feast.*

½ POUND PLUS 4 TABLESPOONS
BUTTER, SOFTENED

1½ CUPS SUGAR

½ CUP BROWN SUGAR

1½ TEASPOONS MAPLE EXTRACT

6 EGGS

2¼ CUPS CAKE FLOUR

2 TEASPOONS BAKING POWDER

½ TEASPOON SALT

1¼ CUPS CHOPPED WALNUTS

1. Preheat oven to 350°F.

2. Grease and flour or line a 10-inch tube pan with parchment paper. Set aside.

3. In an electric mixer on medium speed, cream butter. Add sugar and brown sugar gradually and beat until light in color. Add maple extract.

4. Add eggs, one at a time, beating well after adding each one.

5. On low speed, add flour, baking powder, and salt mix just until ingredients are incorporated. Scrape down the mixing bowl to be sure batter is well mixed.

6. Fold in walnuts.

7. Pour batter into prepared tube pan. Bake for 50 to 55 minutes, or until a tester comes out with a fine crumb. Remove pan from the oven. Let cake cool in pan on wire rack for 10 to 15 minutes. Carefully remove cake from pan and let cool completely on wire rack.

8. Frost with Maple Glaze (page 56) and serve.

YIELD: ONE 10-INCH CAKE, ABOUT 25 SLICES

# PISTACHIO CAKE

*This hearty and flavorful loaf cake is the ideal companion to a cup of fresh brewed coffee. Its light-green color makes it a natural for St. Patrick's Day.*

| | |
|---|---|
| ½ POUND BUTTER | 1¾ CUPS ALL-PURPOSE FLOUR |
| 1¼ CUPS SUGAR | 1 TEASPOON BAKING POWDER |
| 4 EGGS | 1 CUP CHOPPED PISTACHIOS, TOASTED |
| ½ TEASPOON PISTACHIO EXTRACT (OPTIONAL) | CONFECTIONERS' SUGAR FOR DUSTING |

1. Preheat oven to 350°F.

2. Grease and flour or line a 10 x 6 x 2½-inch loaf pan with parchment paper. Set aside.

3. In an electric mixer on medium speed, cream the butter. Add the sugar and beat until light in color. Add the eggs, one at a time, beating well after adding each one. Add pistachio extract.

4. On low speed, gradually add the flour and baking powder. Mix just until blended. Stir in pistachios.

5. Bake for 55 to 60 minutes, or until a tester comes out with a fine crumb. Remove pan from the oven. Cool cake in pan on wire cooling rack for 10 to 15 minutes. Remove cake from the pan and continue to cool cake on wire rack. Remove and discard parchment. Dust top of cake with confectioners' sugar and serve.

YIELD: ONE LARGE LOAF, ABOUT 12 SLICES

# CLASSIC SPONGE CAKE

*This cake has always been a family favorite. Dress it up with a fancy filling or serve it sliced with fresh berries for the perfect summer dessert. Be sure to use a tube pan with a removable bottom.*

7 EGG WHITES, AT ROOM
TEMPERATURE

1½ CUPS SUGAR

½ TEASPOON CREAM OF TARTAR

½ TEASPOON SALT

7 EGG YOLKS

1 TEASPOON VANILLA EXTRACT

1½ CUPS CAKE FLOUR

¼ CUP COLD WATER

1. Preheat oven to 325°F.

2. In an electric mixer with wire whisk attachment, beat egg whites, ¼ cup of the sugar, cream of tartar, and salt. Start on medium speed, then use high speed until very stiff peaks form, 3 to 4 minutes.

3. In a separate bowl, with an electric mixer on medium speed, beat egg yolks, 1¼ cups sugar, and vanilla. Beat until light in color, 2 to 3 minutes.

4. Add flour and water to egg mixture alternately. Start and end with the flour. Mix just until blended.

5. Using a rubber spatula, fold egg yolk mixture into egg whites. When blended, spoon batter into an ungreased 10-inch tube pan with removable bottom. Spread batter evenly.

6. Bake for 60 to 65 minutes, or until top is golden brown. Remove pan from the oven.

7. Invert tube pan to cool cake, about 1 hour.

8. When cool, carefully remove cake from the pan. Use a sharp knife to loosen the outside of the cake from the sides of the pan.

YIELD: ONE 10-INCH CAKE, APPROXIMATELY 20 SLICES

FOR VARIATIONS AND FILLINGS SEE:

Cannoli Cake, page 69

Tiramisù Cake, page 92

Josephine & Napoleon Cake, page 110

Holiday Eggnog Cake, page 78

---

◆ CAKE MYTH #1 ◆

WHEN WE WERE YOUNG, MY MOM ALWAYS TOLD US NOT TO JUMP AROUND NEAR THE OVEN WHILE A CAKE WAS BAKING. WE WERE ALWAYS TOLD OUR MOVEMENT WOULD CAUSE THE CAKE TO FALL. WHAT AN EX-CUSE TO GET CHILDREN TO BEHAVE! ALTHOUGH MOVEMENT AROUND THE OVEN SHOULDN'T MAKE A DIFFERENCE, DON'T OPEN THE OVEN DURING THE FIRST PART OF BAKING. THIS SUDDEN CHANGE IN TEMPERATURE CAN CAUSE THE CAKE TO FALL.

---

# CHOCOLATE SPONGE CAKE

*This variation of the Classic Sponge Cake is a real winner. It is delicious served plain, or with fresh fruit for a perfect summer dessert. You can get creative, too, by substituting this chocolate sponge in layer cake recipes that use a plain sponge. The sky's the limit!*

7 EGG WHITES, AT ROOM
TEMPERATURE

1½ CUPS SUGAR

½ TEASPOON CREAM OF TARTAR

½ TEASPOON SALT

7 EGG YOLKS

1 TEASPOON VANILLA EXTRACT

1 CUP CAKE FLOUR

½ CUP COCOA

¼ CUP WATER

1. Preheat oven to 325°F.

2. In an electric mixer with wire whisk attachment, beat egg whites, ¼ cup of the sugar, cream of tartar, and salt. Start on medium speed and then increase to high speed until very stiff peaks form, 3 to 4 minutes.

3. In a separate bowl, with an electric mixer on medium speed, beat egg yolks, 1¼ cups sugar, and vanilla. Beat until light in color, 2 to 3 minutes.

4. In a small bowl, combine flour and cocoa. Add this mixture alternately with the water to the egg yolk mixture. Start and end with the flour. Mix just until blended.

5. Using a rubber spatula, fold yolk mixture into egg whites. When thoroughly blended, spoon batter into an ungreased 10-inch tube pan with removable bottom. Spread batter evenly.

6. Bake for 60 to 65 minutes. Remove pan from the oven.

7. Invert tube pan to cool cake for about 1 hour.

8. When cool, use a sharp knife to loosen the cake from the pan.

YIELD: ONE 10-INCH CAKE, ABOUT 20 SLICES

# CHOCOLATE ALMOND
# ANGEL FOOD CAKE

*This is a new twist on the classic angel food cake. Angel food cakes have always been popular for their light texture and have always been a great fat-free choice for dessert. For a low-fat filled Mocha Cake, see page 114.*

| | |
|---|---|
| ¾ CUPS CAKE FLOUR | ¼ TEASPOON SALT |
| 4 TABLESPOONS COCOA | 1 TEASPOON CREAM OF TARTAR |
| 1¼ CUPS SUGAR | 1 TEASPOON ALMOND EXTRACT |
| 10 EGG WHITES | CONFECTIONERS' SUGAR FOR DUSTING |

1. Preheat oven to 325°F.

2. In a small bowl, combine flour, cocoa, and ¼ cup of the sugar. Set aside

3. In an electric mixer with wire whisk attachment, beat egg whites and salt. When foamy, add cream of tartar. Whip until stiff peaks form.

4. Add remaining sugar gradually, 2 tablespoons at a time. Mix until blended.

5. Fold in almond extract. Carefully fold flour mixture into egg white mixture just until ingredients are incorporated.

6. Pour batter onto an ungreased 10-inch tube pan. Bake for 40 to 45 minutes. Remove pan from oven. Invert cake to cool pan for about 1 hour. Carefully remove cake from pan.

7. Dust with confectioners' sugar and serve.

YIELD: ONE 10-INCH CAKE, ABOUT 15 SLICES

---

◆ ANGEL VS. DEVIL'S FOOD ◆

THESE CAKES WERE PROBABLY NAMED TO REPRESENT THE GOOD AND EVIL IN THE WORLD. ANGEL FOOD WAS MEANT TO BE LIGHT AND HEAVENLY AND PURE IN COLOR, WHEREAS DEVIL'S FOOD IS RICH, DENSE, AND NOT AS GOOD FOR YOU. HAPPILY, YOU DON'T HAVE TO CHOOSE JUST ONE. . . .

# CAPPUCCINO CHIFFON CAKE

*This light and fluffy cake has a nice coffee flavor with a hint of cinnamon. You can dust the top with confectioners' sugar, or try a slice with a scoop of coffee ice cream and a drizzle of hot fudge sauce.*

| | |
|---|---|
| 6 EGGS, SEPARATED | 2 TEASPOONS COFFEE LIQUEUR |
| ½ TEASPOON CREAM OF TARTAR | 2¼ CUPS CAKE FLOUR |
| 1¼ CUPS SUGAR | 3 TEASPOONS BAKING POWDER |
| ¾ CUPS COOLED BREWED ESPRESSO | 2 TEASPOONS CINNAMON |
| ½ CUP VEGETABLE OIL | |

1. Preheat oven to 325°F.

2. In an electric mixer with wire attachment, beat egg whites, cream of tartar, and ½ cup of the sugar until stiff peaks form. Set aside.

3. In an electric mixer on medium speed, beat egg yolks. Gradually add remaining sugar. Add espresso, vegetable oil, and coffee liqueur. On low speed, gradually add the flour, baking powder, and cinnamon. Mix until smooth. Using a rubber spatula, carefully fold flour mixture into egg whites. Pour batter into an un-greased 10-inch tube pan.

4. Bake for 50 to 55 minutes, or until a tester comes out clean. Remove cake from the oven. Invert cake to cool for about 1 hour. When completely cool, carefully remove cake from the pan. Using a sharp knife, loosen cake from around the sides and center of the pan.

YIELD: ONE 10-INCH CAKE, ABOUT 20 SLICES

# APPLESAUCE CAKE

*This is another personal favorite. It's easy to make and is just as popular eaten for breakfast, an afternoon snack, or dessert after a potluck supper.*

| | |
|---|---|
| 4 TABLESPOONS BUTTER, SOFTENED | 1¼ CUPS ALL-PURPOSE FLOUR |
| ½ CUP SUGAR | 1 TEASPOON BAKING SODA |
| 1 EGG | ½ TEASPOON BAKING POWDER |
| 1 TEASPOON VANILLA EXTRACT | ½ TEASPOON CINNAMON |
| 1 CUP CHUNKY APPLESAUCE | |

1. Preheat oven to 350°F.

2. Grease and flour or line an 8 x 4 x 3-inch loaf pan with parchment paper. Set aside.

3. In an electric mixer on medium speed, cream the butter. Add the sugar and beat until light. Add the egg, vanilla, and applesauce. Beat until well blended.

4. On low speed, gradually add the flour, baking soda, baking powder, and cinnamon. Mix just until blended. Pour batter into prepared pan.

5. Bake for 45 to 50 minutes, or until a tester comes out with a fine crumb. Remove pan from the oven. Cool cake in pan on wire rack for 10 to 15 minutes. Remove cake from the pan and continue to cool on wire rack.

YIELD: ONE SMALL LOAF, ABOUT 10 SLICES

# ORANGE PLUM CAKE

*This cake has a tender texture and combines fresh and dried fruit. The tart dried plums add a nice contrast to the sweetness of the orange. Perfect for breakfast or afternoon tea.*

¼ POUND PLUS 3 TABLESPOONS BUTTER, SOFTENED

1 CUP CONFECTIONERS' SUGAR

2 EGGS

½ TEASPOON VANILLA EXTRACT

1 CUP CAKE FLOUR

½ TEASPOON BAKING POWDER

GRATED RIND OF 1 ORANGE

1 ORANGE, PEELED AND CUT INTO SMALL PIECES

1 CUP DRIED PLUMS, COARSELY CHOPPED

CONFECTIONERS' SUGAR FOR DUSTING

1. Preheat oven to 350°F.

2. Grease and flour or line a 10 x 6 x 2½-inch loaf pan with parchment paper. Set aside.

3. In an electric mixer on medium speed, cream the butter and confectioners' sugar until blended. Scrape down the sides of the bowl with a rubber spatula.

4. Add the eggs, one at a time, beating well after each egg. Add vanilla.

5. On low speed, gradually add the flour, baking powder, and orange rind. Mix just until blended.

6. Stir in orange pieces and plums. Spoon batter into prepared pan.

7. Bake for 50 to 55 minutes, or until a tester comes out with a fine crumb. Remove pan from the oven.

8. Cool cake in pan on wire rack for 10 to 15 minutes. Remove from the pan. Continue cooling cake on wire rack until cool. Remove and discard parchment. Dust the top with confectioners' sugar.

9. Store cake at room temperature, wrapped in aluminum foil or plastic wrap. Or freeze for later use.

YIELD: ONE LARGE LOAF, ABOUT 12 SLICES

# CHOCOLATE MINT CAKE

*This cake has a subtle chocolate flavor, accented with fresh mint, which is usually available year-round in most supermarkets. Our local herb farm also has a nice chocolate mint plant that works wonderfully in this recipe.*

| | |
|---|---|
| ½ POUND BUTTER | 2 TEASPOONS BAKING POWDER |
| 3 CUPS SUGAR | ¼ TEASPOON SALT |
| 3 TABLESPOONS INSTANT COFFEE | 1 CUP COCOA |
| 2 TEASPOONS COFFEE LIQUEUR | 1¾ CUPS BUTTERMILK |
| 3 EGGS | 2 TABLESPOONS FRESH MINT LEAVES |
| 3 CUPS CAKE FLOUR | |

1. Preheat oven to 350°F.

2. Grease and flour or line a 10-inch tube pan with parchment paper. Set aside.

3. In an electric mixer on medium speed, cream the butter. Gradually add the sugar and beat until light in color. Add coffee and liqueur. Add the eggs, one at a time, beating well after adding each one.

4. In a medium bowl, combine flour, baking powder, salt, and cocoa. Add this flour mixture to the butter mixture alternately with the buttermilk, beginning and ending with the flour mixture. Stir in mint leaves. Mix just until blended. Pour batter into prepared pan.

5. Bake for 1 hour and 10 minutes, or until a tester comes out with a fine crumb. Remove cake from the oven and cool in pan on wire cooling rack for 10 to 15 minutes.

6. Carefully remove cake from the pan and continue to cool on wire rack. Remove and discard parchment. Serve, or store at room temperature in foil.

YIELD: ONE 10-INCH CAKE, ABOUT 25 SLICES

# FIG COFFEE CAKE

*Another family favorite—a delicious butter cake accented by a rich fig-and-raspberry filling. This recipe makes two large loaf cakes, one to serve now, another for the freezer or a friend.*

**FILLING:**

| | |
|---|---|
| 12 OUNCES DRIED FIGS | 2 TABLESPOONS GRAND MARNIER |
| ½ CUP SUGAR | ½ CUP CHOPPED WALNUTS |
| 1 TEASPOON CINNAMON | ½ CUP RASPBERRY PRESERVES |

**CAKE:**

| | |
|---|---|
| ½ POUND BUTTER, SOFTENED | 3 CUPS ALL-PURPOSE FLOUR |
| 3 CUPS SUGAR | ¼ TEASPOON BAKING SODA |
| 2 TEASPOONS VANILLA EXTRACT | 1 CUP SOUR CREAM |
| 6 EGGS | |

1. Place figs in a medium saucepan. Cover with water. Boil, uncovered, on high heat until tender, about 10 minutes. Drain.

2. Pour figs into food processor and process until finely chopped. Place in a small bowl. Stir in sugar, cinnamon, Grand Marnier, nuts, and raspberry preserves. Set aside.

3. Preheat oven to 350°F. Grease and flour or line two 10 x 6 x 2½-inch loaf pans with baking parchment. Set aside.

4. In an electric mixer on medium speed, cream butter. Add sugar and beat until light. Add vanilla. Add the eggs, one at a time, beating well after each egg.

5. Combine flour and baking soda. On low speed, add flour mixture to the butter mixture alternately with sour cream. Start and end with the flour mixture. Mix just until blended.

6. Pour half the batter into prepared pans. Spread half the filling over the batter. Pour remaining batter evenly over two cakes. Spoon remaining filling evenly over two cakes. Bake for 75 to 80 minutes, or until a tester comes out with a fine crumb. Remove pans from the oven.

7. Place on wire cooling rack and cool cakes in pans for 15 to 20 minutes. Carefully remove cakes from the pans and place on wire cooling rack to cool. Remove and discard parchment.

YIELD: TWO LARGE LOAVES, ABOUT 12 SLICES EACH

---

◆ COFFEE CAKES ◆

THIS TERM ORIGINALLY REFERRED TO CAKES THAT WERE MADE WITH YEAST, SIMILAR TO A DANISH ROLL. TODAY, IT'S USED TO INCLUDE ANY TYPE OF RICH CAKE FILLED WITH FRUIT, NUTS, OR CHEESE.

---

# CINNAMON SOUR CREAM CAKE

*This is truly one of my all-time favorites. The cinnamon-and-sugar filling is perfect anywhere and anytime—breakfasts, picnics, or lunches. Plus, baking this cake makes the whole house smell good.*

**FILLING:**

½ CUP SUGAR

2 TEASPOONS CINNAMON

½ CUP WALNUTS, FINELY CHOPPED

**CAKE:**

¼ POUND BUTTER, SOFTENED

1 CUP SUGAR

3 EGGS

1 CUP SOUR CREAM

1 TEASPOON ALMOND EXTRACT

1 TEASPOON VANILLA EXTRACT

3 CUPS CAKE FLOUR

3 TEASPOONS BAKING POWDER

1 TEASPOON BAKING SODA

½ TEASPOON SALT

1. Preheat oven to 350°F.

2. Grease and flour or line a 10-inch tube pan with parchment paper. Set aside.

3. For the filling, combine sugar, cinnamon, and walnuts in a small bowl. Set aside.

4. Using an electric mixer on medium speed, cream the butter and sugar until light in color. Add eggs, one at a time, beating well after adding each egg. Add sour cream and almond and vanilla extracts.

5. On low speed, gradually add flour, baking powder, baking soda, and salt. Mix just until blended.

6. Spread half the batter in the prepared tube pan. Sprinkle the batter with three quarters of the filling mixture. Spread remaining batter on top of filling. Sprinkle top of cake with remaining filling.

7. Bake for 50 to 60 minutes, or until a tester comes out with a fine crumb. Remove pan from the oven. Place on a wire cooling rack. Cool cake in pan for 10 to 15 minutes. Carefully remove cake from the pan and continue cooling on wire rack. Remove and discard parchment.

**8.** Slice and serve warm, or cool completely and wrap in foil. Store at room temperature.

YIELD: ONE 10-INCH CAKE, ABOUT 20 SLICES

# SPECKLED CHIP POUND CAKE

*This cake combines the best white and dark chocolate flavors with chopped walnuts. It is ideal served slightly warm with ice cream and a drizzle of chocolate sauce.*

| | |
|---|---|
| ¾ CUP WHITE CHOCOLATE CHIPS | 3 EGGS |
| ¾ CUP SEMISWEET CHOCOLATE CHIPS | 2½ CUPS ALL-PURPOSE FLOUR |
| 1 CUP WALNUTS, FINELY CHOPPED | ½ TEASPOON BAKING SODA |
| ½ POUND BUTTER, SOFTENED | ¼ TEASPOON SALT |
| 2 CUPS SUGAR | 1 CUP BUTTERMILK |
| 1 TEASPOON VANILLA EXTRACT | |

1. Preheat oven to 350°F.

2. Grease and flour a 10-inch Bundt pan. Set aside.

3. In a food processor, pulse chocolate chips and nuts until very fine. Set aside.

4. In an electric mixer on medium speed, cream the butter. Gradually add the sugar and beat until light in color. Add vanilla. Add eggs, one at a time, beating well after adding each egg. Mix until well blended.

5. In a small bowl, combine flour, baking soda, and salt. On low speed, add flour mixture, alternately with buttermilk. Start and end with the flour mixture. Mix just until blended.

6. Stir in chocolate chips and nuts until well blended. Pour batter into prepared pan.

7. Bake for 60 to 65 minutes, or until a tester comes out with a fine crumb. Remove pan from the oven. Cool in pan on wire cooling rack for 10 to 15 minutes. Carefully remove cake from the pan and continue cooling on wire rack, fluted side up, until cool. Drizzle with Chocolate Glaze (page 55) and serve with a scoop of ice cream.

YIELD: ONE 10-INCH CAKE, 20 TO 25 SLICES

# SWEET POTATO CAKE

*Sweet potatoes or yams can be used interchangeably in this and many recipes. Sweet potatoes are not really related to the potato family but are members of the root vegetable family. They have always been a popular ingredient in Southern cooking and add a nice flavor and texture to this cake.*

| | |
|---|---|
| 4 EGGS | 2 TEASPOONS BAKING POWDER |
| 2 CUPS SUGAR | 2 TEASPOONS CINNAMON |
| 1¼ CUP VEGETABLE OIL | ½ TEASPOON CLOVES |
| 1 TEASPOON VANILLA EXTRACT | 2 CUPS GRATED SWEET POTATO |
| 3 CUPS ALL-PURPOSE FLOUR | 1 CUP WALNUTS, COARSELY CHOPPED |
| 2 TEASPOONS BAKING SODA | |

1. Preheat oven to 350°F.

2. Grease and flour or line a 10-inch tube pan with parchment paper. Set aside.

3. In an electric mixer on medium speed, blend together eggs, sugar, oil, and vanilla. Mix until well blended. On low speed, gradually add flour, baking soda, baking powder, cinnamon and cloves. Mix just until blended and smooth. Stir in sweet potato and walnuts.

4. Pour into prepared pan and bake for 55 to 60 minutes. Remove from the oven and place on wire cooling rack. Cool in pan for 10 to 15 minutes. Remove cake from the pan and continue cooling on wire rack until completely cool. Remove and discard parchment.

5. Frost with Maple Glaze (page 56) and serve.

YIELD: ONE 10-INCH CAKE, 20 TO 25 SLICES

# PEAR, NUT & RAISIN LOAF

*This twist on a traditional pound cake spotlights the growing popularity of pears. Bosc pears are the best for flavor and texture in baking, and they're available year-round. This moist cake, loaded with pears, raisins, and walnuts, is perfectly appropriate at breakfast or at the dinner table with assorted breads, or as dessert, topped with ice cream.*

| | |
|---|---|
| 2 BOSC PEARS | ¼ TEASPOON SALT |
| ¼ POUND BUTTER, SOFTENED | 1 TEASPOON CINNAMON |
| 1½ CUPS SUGAR | 1 TEASPOON NUTMEG |
| 1 TEASPOON VANILLA EXTRACT | 2 PEARS, PEELED, CORED, AND DICED (ABOUT 1½ CUPS) |
| 4 EGGS | 1 CUP RAISINS |
| 2½ CUPS CAKE FLOUR | 1 CUP CHOPPED WALNUTS |
| 1 TEASPOON BAKING POWDER | |

1. Peel and core the two Bosc pears and cut into ½-inch slices. Put pears in a small saucepan and cover with water. Boil, uncovered, over high heat for 15 to 20 minutes, or until tender. Drain. Purée in a food processor until the consistency of applesauce. You should have 1 cup. Set aside.

2. Preheat oven to 350°F.

3. Grease and flour or line a 10 x 6 x 2½-inch loaf pan with parchment paper. Set aside.

4. In an electric mixer on medium speed, cream the butter. Gradually add the sugar, beating until light in color. Add the 1 cup pear purée and vanilla. Mix until blended.

5. Add eggs, one at a time, beating well after adding each one.

6. On low speed, gradually add flour, baking powder, salt, cinnamon, and nutmeg. Mix just until blended. Stir in diced pears, raisins, and nuts. Pour batter into prepared pan.

7. Bake for 55 to 60 minutes, or until a tester comes out with a fine crumb. Remove cake from the oven and cool in a pan on wire cooling rack for 10 to 15 minutes.

8. Carefully remove the cake from the pan and continue to cool on wire cooling rack. Remove and discard parchment. Serve slightly warm or wrap in foil and store at room temperature.

YIELD: ONE LARGE LOAF, ABOUT 12 SLICES

# LEMON ROSEMARY CAKE

*This cake has an unusual texture because of the cornmeal added to the flour.*
*It is a slightly sweet cake, accented by fresh rosemary,*
*that is nice with a summer soup or salad.*

¼ POUND PLUS 3 TABLESPOONS
BUTTER, SOFTENED

1½ CUPS SUGAR

4 EGGS

2 CUPS CAKE FLOUR

½ CUP YELLOW CORNMEAL

½ TEASPOON SALT

2 TEASPOONS BAKING POWDER

½ CUP WHITE WINE

GRATED RIND OF 1 LEMON

2 TABLESPOONS MINCED ROSEMARY

GLAZE:

¼ CUP WHITE WINE

JUICE OF 1 LEMON

1. Preheat oven to 325°F.

2. Grease and flour or line a 10 x 6 x 2½-inch loaf pan with parchment paper. Set aside.

3. In an electric mixer on medium speed, cream butter. Gradually add sugar and beat until light in color. Add eggs, one at a time, beating well after adding each one.

4. On low speed, add flour, cornmeal, salt, and baking powder. Mix just until blended. Add wine. Stir in lemon rind and rosemary. Pour batter into prepared pan.

5. Bake for 60 to 65 minutes, or until a tester comes out with a fine crumb. Remove cake from the oven and cool on wire cooling rack.

6. In a small bowl, stir together wine and lemon juice. Pour evenly over the top of the cake. Cool in pan on wire cooling rack for 10 to 15 minutes. Carefully remove the cake from the pan and continue to cool on wire rack. Remove and discard parchment. Serve when cool, or wrap in foil for storage at room temperature or freezing.

YIELD: ONE LARGE LOAF, ABOUT 12 SLICES

# LESS-GUILT ORANGE CAKE

*Margarine replaces some of the fat of butter in this lightly flavored cake. Egg whites add volume, and orange rind provides a subtle orange flavor, for a cake with a little less guilt. It's the perfect companion to a glass of iced herbal tea on a summer day.*

| | |
|---|---|
| 4 EGG WHITES | 1½ CUPS CAKE FLOUR |
| ¼ POUND MARGARINE, SOFTENED | 2 TEASPOONS BAKING POWDER |
| 1 CUP SUGAR | ½ TEASPOON SALT |
| 4 TABLESPOONS ORANGE JUICE | ¾ CUP BUTTERMILK |
| 1 TABLESPOON GRATED ORANGE RIND | CONFECTIONERS' SUGAR FOR DUSTING |
| 1 TEASPOON VANILLA EXTRACT | |

1. Preheat oven to 350°F.

2. Grease and flour or line a 10 x 6 x 2½-inch loaf pan with parchment paper. Set aside.

3. In an electric mixer, with a wire whisk, whip egg whites until stiff. Set aside.

4. With an electric mixer on medium speed, blend margarine and sugar until light in color. Add 2 tablespoons of the orange juice, rind, and vanilla. Blend well.

5. In a small bowl, combine flour, baking powder, and salt. Add to margarine mixture alternately with buttermilk. Mix just until blended. Fold batter mixture into the beaten egg whites. Pour into prepared pan.

6. Bake for 45 to 50 minutes, or until a tester comes out with a fine crumb. Remove cake from the oven and place on wire cooling rack. Pour 2 tablespoons of orange juice on top of baked cake. Cool cake in pan for 10 to 15 minutes. Remove cake from pan and continue to cool on wire cooling rack until completely cool. Remove and discard parchment.

7. Dust with confectioners' sugar and serve topped with fresh fruit.

YIELD: ONE LARGE LOAF, ABOUT 12 SLICES

# MINI CHOCOLATE MOCHA LOAVES

*These tiny chocolate-coated cakes make great individual desserts, served alone or on a plate with Raspberry Sauce (page 58). We originally created them as wedding favors. They were miniature monogrammed versions of the wedding cake that made the perfect take-home treat. For these cakes you will need miniature loaf pans. They are usually sold in sets of six and measure 4 x 2 x 1½ inches each.*

ONE RECIPE DEVIL'S FOOD LAYER CAKE   ONE RECIPE CHOCOLATE GANACHE
(PAGE 67)                            (PAGE 123)

ONE RECIPE MOCHA MOUSSE FILLING
(PAGE 82)

1. Preheat oven to 350°F.

2. Prepare cake batter according to directions. Grease and flour mini loaf pans. Fill pans halfway with batter. Bake for 12 to 15 minutes, or until done.

3. Remove pans from the oven. Carefully remove cakes from the pans and place on wire cooling rack. To reuse the pans, be sure to clean in between uses. If the pans are not cleaned properly after baking the first batch, the second batch of cakes may stick and become difficult to remove.

4. Grease and flour pans and repeat, filling pans halfway with remaining batter. Bake until done. Cool cakes completely on wire cooling rack.

5. Prepare Mocha Mousse.

6. Fill a pastry bag, fitted with an open star tip, with mocha mousse. Push the tip of the pastry bag into the bottom of the cake at 3 intervals. Squeeze pastry bag gently to release the filling into the cake. Be careful not to push the tip too far in or squeeze too much filling or you might break the cake. Re-fill the pastry bag as necessary and fill all 12 cakes.

7. Place filled cakes, bottoms down, on a wire rack. Use a clean piece of parchment or waxed paper under the wire rack to catch any excess ganache.

8. Prepare ganache. Let cool until lukewarm.

9. Using a tablespoon, pour ganache over mini loaves, one at a time. Use the back of the spoon or a metal spatula to smooth ganache over the top and onto the sides of the cake. Glaze all the cakes with ganache.

**10.** Refrigerate cakes until set. Let cakes come to room temperature before serving.

YIELD: TWELVE MINIATURE LOAVES, ABOUT 12 SERVINGS

---

◆ **BAKERY STORIES** ◆

AT SWEET MARIA'S, WE'VE MADE QUITE A FEW INTERESTING CAKES.
SOME OF THE MOST MEMORABLE ARE: A CAKE THAT REPLICATES A TERRA-
COTTA POT, WITH FLOWERS; A FOOD-COLORING-PAINTED MING BOWL; A
MOUNTAIN RANGE WEDDING CAKE, COMPLETE WITH SNOW-CAPPED TOPS;
CAKES SHAPED LIKE A PLATFORM SHOE, A SMALL PIANO, A JEWELRY BOX,
TACKY SUNGLASSES; AND NUMEROUS OTHER HOLIDAY AND WEDDING
CREATIONS. WE'VE ALSO DONE DIVORCE CAKES, "WILL YOU MARRY ME?"
CAKES, AND CAKES FOR DOG BIRTHDAYS. OUR CAKES ARE AS VARIED AND
UNIQUE AS OUR CUSTOMERS ARE.

---

# CONFECTIONERS' GLAZE

*Besides being perfect for loaf and Bundt cakes, this basic glaze can be used on cookies,*
*layer cakes, or danish pastries. You can substitute almost any flavor extract, including*
*vanilla or almond, to make a variety of confectioners' glazes.*

**3 CUPS CONFECTIONERS' SUGAR**          **¼ CUP WATER**
**1 TEASPOON LEMON EXTRACT**

Using an electric mixer, blend sugar, lemon extract, and water until blended.
Beat on medium speed until smooth. Use a metal spatula to spread on the top of
the cake. Place cake on wire rack, set on clean parchment to allow for easy
cleanup of excess icing. Use immediately or cover and store at room temperature
for later use.

**YIELD: ENOUGH TO GLAZE THE TOP OF ONE 10-INCH TUBE CAKE OR 2 LARGE LOAVES**

# CHOCOLATE CONFECTIONERS' GLAZE

*A rich glaze ideal to drizzle over the top of a pound cake.*

1½ CUPS CONFECTIONERS' SUGAR          ¼ CUP WATER

¼ CUP COCOA

Using an electric mixer, blend sugar, cocoa, and water together until blended. Beat on medium speed until smooth. Use a metal spatula to spread glaze over the top of the cake. Use immediately.

YIELD: ENOUGH TO GLAZE THE TOP OF A 10-INCH TUBE CAKE OR TWO LARGE LOAVES

# MAPLE GLAZE

*This glaze is great on some of our spicier cakes. Try it drizzled over the New England Maple Walnut Cake, Sweet Potato Cake, or Pear, Nut & Raisin Loaf.*

**1½ CUPS CONFECTIONERS' SUGAR          ½ CUP MAPLE SYRUP**

In an electric mixer, blend confectioners' sugar and maple syrup until blended and smooth. Use a metal spatula to spread glaze over the top of the cake. Use immediately.

**YIELD: ENOUGH TO GLAZE THE TOP OF A 10-INCH TUBE CAKE OR TWO LARGE LOAVES**

# WHIPPED CREAM

*Sometimes the best garnish for a slice of cake is a dollop of whipped cream. If you're using the cream this way, it doesn't need to be as stiff as if you were frosting a layer cake.*

**1 CUP HEAVY CREAM**　　　　　　　**2 TABLESPOONS SUGAR**

In an electric mixer with wire whip attachment, beat cream into peaks, about 2 minutes. Whisk in sugar. Beat until stiff, about another 30 seconds. Use immediately.

**YIELD: 2 CUPS**

# RASPBERRY SAUCE

*This sauce is the perfect partner to any chocolate or lemon cake.*

**2 CUPS FROZEN (SLIGHTLY THAWED)**
**OR FRESH RASPBERRIES**

**1 CUP CONFECTIONERS' SUGAR**

Place berries and sugar in a food processor. Process until puréed and almost smooth. Use immediately or refrigerate in an airtight container.

**YIELD: 1½ CUPS**

# STRAWBERRIES IN VERMOUTH

*This is one of my grandmother's specialties. It's ideal simply spooned over a slice of sponge cake or on top of a slice of pound cake with ice cream.*

1 QUART FRESH STRAWBERRIES,
CLEANED, HULLED, AND SLICED

1 CUP SWEET VERMOUTH

½ CUP SUGAR

1. Place berries in a small mixing bowl. Pour vermouth over strawberries and sprinkle with sugar. Stir with a rubber spatula.

2. Cover and refrigerate overnight. Serve chilled, spooned over cake and ice cream.

YIELD: ABOUT 15 ½-CUP SERVINGS TO USE IMMEDIATELY OR FREEZE

# LAYER CAKES

*All of these layer cakes have three elements: cake, filling, and frosting. Read through each recipe before you start so that you can have a good idea when to make each element. Many of the cakes can be baked one day in advance. Custard fillings and buttercream frostings are best made one day ahead. Whipped cream and seven-minute frostings need to be whipped right before assembly of your cake.*
*They cannot be saved and used later.*

### *How to Slice Cakes Horizontally to Fill Them*

If you're making a two-layer cake, be sure to level off the tops of the layers by carefully slicing with a long sharp serrated knife. With one hand on the top, use a slow sawing motion to be sure you can control the knife and not slice your hand. If you don't level off the tops of your layers, you will have a rounded cake top, which is more likely to crack.

To slice two layers into four layers, use the same motion to split the layer as you would to slice off the top. If the layers are thin and fragile, use a wire cooling rack or cake circle to help move the layer during assembly.

## Adhering Cakes to Plates

It is very important that you properly adhere your cake to its serving plate or cake circle. If the cake is not secure, it may slide off the plate. If you're using a buttercream frosting, use a dab of frosting to act as glue—it works quite well. Place a dab of frosting on the plate or cake circle. Gently press a doily to adhere to plate. Place another dab of frosting on the doily. Gently press the bottom cake layer onto this dab. If you're making a whipped cream–frosted cake, it's a good idea to use a bit of buttercream or confectioners' icing for this purpose.

## Frosting and Garnishing

Many of these cakes use simple swirled frostings that are spread with a metal spatula. I've tried to make this book "decorator friendly" by showing easy ways to cover cakes and garnish for a pretty presentation.

# WHITE LAYER CAKE

*This is a versatile cake with a light texture and flavor. It works with any number of frostings, fresh fruit, and whipped cream or a sweet buttercream. This recipe uses only egg whites. If you're making the Lemon Curd Filling (page 80), you can use the yolks for that.*

| | |
|---|---|
| 2½ CUPS CAKE FLOUR | 5 EGG WHITES |
| 1½ CUPS SUGAR | 1 CUP MILK |
| 3 TEASPOONS BAKING POWDER | 1 TEASPOON VANILLA EXTRACT |
| ½ TEASPOON SALT | |
| ¼ POUND PLUS 3 TABLESPOONS BUTTER, SOFTENED | |

1. Preheat oven to 350°F.

2. Grease and flour or line two 8-inch round cake pans with parchment paper. Set aside.

3. In an electric mixer on low speed, blend flour, sugar, baking powder, and salt until mixed. Add butter and mix until butter is uniformly blended.

4. In a separate bowl, mix egg whites, milk, and vanilla with a wire whisk.

5. Add egg mixture to flour mixture. Mix on medium speed for 1 minute.

6. Scrape down the sides of the mixing bowl. Continue to beat at medium-high speed for another minute, until batter is blended and smooth.

7. Pour batter evenly into prepared pans. Bake for 25 to 30 minutes, or until a tester comes out with a fine crumb.

8. Remove pans from the oven and cool the cakes in pans on wire cooling racks for 5 to 10 minutes. Carefully remove the cakes from the pans and continue to cool on wire racks. Remove and discard parchment.

YIELD: TWO 8-INCH ROUND LAYERS OR 20 CUPCAKES

# POPPYSEED CAKE

Add ¼ cup poppyseeds to batter.

# ALMOND CAKE

Replace vanilla with 1 teaspoon almond extract.

---

## ◆ OTHER VARIATIONS ◆

Most of the serving suggestions in this book are just that—suggestions. Feel free to make your own combinations using the basics in this book. Here are a few variations to help you get started:

Almond pound cake drizzled with raspberry sauce.

Pumpkin raisin cake or sweet potato cake with a dollop of spiced whipped cream frosting.

Chocolate almond angel food cake with fresh berries and whipped cream.

Speckled pound cake served warm with a scoop of ice cream.

Citrus yogurt cake with fresh berries and raspberry sauce.

A boston creme cake: yellow layer cake, vanilla custard filling, and chocolate frosting.

Chip & ernie's cake using white chocolate chips and buttercream frosting.

Banana sour cream cake with cream cheese frosting.

Devil's food cake with seven-minute frosting covered with coconut.

Banana sour cream cake with mocha mousse filling and ganache.

Try apricot preserves instead of raspberry in the hazelnut cake.

---

# YELLOW LAYER CAKE

*This flexible recipe is the basis for many of the layer cake variations included in this chapter. By beating the egg whites separately, then folding them into the batter, you get a very light and flavorful cake.*

4 EGGS, SEPARATED

½ POUND BUTTER, SOFTENED

2 CUPS SUGAR

1 TEASPOON VANILLA EXTRACT

2½ CUPS CAKE FLOUR

2 TEASPOONS BAKING POWDER

¼ TEASPOON SALT

1 CUP MILK

1. Preheat oven to 350°F.

2. Grease and flour or line two 9-inch round cake pans with parchment paper. Set aside.

3. In an electric mixer with wire whisk attachment, beat egg whites until soft but not dry. Set aside.

4. In an electric mixer on medium speed, cream the butter. Gradually add sugar and beat until light in color. Add vanilla. Add egg yolks, one at a time, beating well after adding each one.

5. In another bowl, combine flour, baking powder, and salt. Add the flour mixture to the butter mixture alternately with the milk. Begin and end with flour mixture. Mix until batter is smooth.

6. Carefully fold flour mixture into egg whites.

7. Pour batter into prepared pans. Bake for 25 to 30 minutes, or until a tester comes out with a fine crumb. Remove pans from the oven and place on a wire cooling rack. Cool cakes in pans for 5 to 10 minutes. Carefully remove cakes from the pans and continue to cool on wire racks. Remove and discard parchment before decorating.

8. When cool, frost as desired or wrap in foil and freeze.

YIELD: TWO 9-INCH ROUND LAYERS OR 24 CUPCAKES

# DEVIL'S FOOD LAYER CAKE

*This amazing cake can't be beat for moistness or flavor. It is also very flexible. You can use this recipe for our chocolate layer cakes or for our Mini Chocolate Mocha Loaves.*

| | |
|---|---|
| 1 CUP COCOA | 1 TEASPOON SALT |
| 1 CUP BOILING WATER | 2 EGGS |
| 2 CUPS FLOUR | 1 CUP BUTTERMILK |
| 1 ¾ CUPS SUGAR | ½ CUP VEGETABLE OIL |
| 1 ½ TEASPOONS BAKING SODA | 2 TEASPOONS VANILLA EXTRACT |
| 2 TEASPOONS BAKING POWDER | |

1. In a small bowl, pour boiling water over cocoa. Set aside to cool.

2. Preheat oven to 350°F.

3. Grease and flour or line two 9-inch round cake pans with parchment paper. Set aside.

4. In an electric mixer, combine flour, sugar, baking soda, baking powder, and salt. Mix on low speed until mixed.

5. Add eggs and cocoa mixture and blend on low speed 1 minute. Scrape down the sides and bottom of mixing bowl.

6. Add buttermilk, oil, and vanilla. Beat on low speed 1 minute. Scrape down bowl. Beat on medium speed for 1 to 2 minutes, or until smooth. Pour batter evenly into prepared pans.

7. Bake for 20 to 25 minutes, or until a tester comes out with a fine crumb. Remove pans from the oven and place on wire cooling racks. Cool cakes in pans for 5 to 10 minutes. Carefully remove cakes from the pans and place on wire cooling racks.

8. Cool completely before frosting. Remove and discard parchment before decorating. Store unfrosted layers wrapped in foil, then plastic, in the freezer.

YIELD: TWO 9-INCH ROUND LAYERS, 12 MINI LOAF CAKES, OR 24 CUPCAKES

# CHOCOLATE STRAWBERRY VALENTINE CAKE

*This heart-shaped devil's food cake is filled with a light strawberry cream filling. It's the perfect ending to a romantic dinner. Or for a great Valentine surprise, bake one and deliver it to your sweetheart at work.*

TWO 9-INCH HEART-SHAPED LAYERS DEVIL'S FOOD CAKE (PAGE 67)

1 RECIPE STRAWBERRY CREAM FILLING (RECIPE FOLLOWS)

1 RECIPE CHOCOLATE BUTTERCREAM (PAGE 120)

GARNISH: CHOCOLATE-DIPPED STRAW-BERRIES

## STRAWBERRY CREAM FILLING

2 CUPS HEAVY CREAM

1 CUP STRAWBERRY PRESERVES

In an electric mixer with wire whisk attachment, whip cream until almost stiff. Add preserves and whip on high speed until stiff. Use immediately.

ASSEMBLY:

1. Make cake layers and chocolate buttercream frosting. Set frosting aside at room temperature in an airtight container or in a bowl covered with plastic wrap.

2. Make strawberry cream filling.

3. Level off tops of the cake layers. Slice each layer horizontally to give you 4 thin layers. Adhere one layer, cut side up, on a serving plate or doily-covered cake circle. Using a pastry bag filled with chocolate buttercream frosting, pipe an outline around the outside of the layer. Fill with a thin layer of the strawberry cream. Repeat with 2 layers and filling until entire cake is filled. Place last layer, cut side down, on top. Refrigerate cake for 10 to 15 minutes.

4. Frost the outside of the cake with remaining chocolate buttercream frosting. Using a metal spatula, start at the top and spread the frosting to cover the sides of the cake. If desired, pipe a border along the bottom edge of the cake. Garnish with chocolate-dipped strawberries or fresh flowers. Refrigerate cake. Serve at room temperature.

YIELD: ONE 4-LAYER 9-INCH HEART-SHAPED CAKE, 15 TO 18 SERVINGS

# CANNOLI CAKE

*This three-layer cake pays tribute to the classic Italian pastry. It's a light sponge cake with a sweetened ricotta cheese filling, sprinkled with a few chocolate chips. It makes a perfect dessert after a traditional Italian pasta supper, with a cup of espresso.*

1 CLASSIC SPONGE CAKE (BAKED IN A10-INCH TUBE PAN (PAGE 34)

1 RECIPE CANNOLI FILLING (RECIPE FOLLOWS)

1 RECIPE WHIPPED CREAM FROSTING (PAGE 122)

GARNISH: ¼ CUP MINI CHOCOLATE CHIPS

## CANNOLI FILLING

3 CUPS WHOLE MILK RICOTTA

½ CUP SUGAR

2 TEASPOONS LEMON EXTRACT

½ CUP MINI CHOCOLATE CHIPS

Combine ricotta, sugar, and lemon extract in a mixing bowl. Stir with a rubber spatula until blended. Stir in chocolate chips. Use immediately or store refrigerated in an airtight container.

**ASSEMBLY:**

1. Cut sponge cake into thirds, horizontally. Place the bottom layer, cut side up, on a serving dish or doily-covered cake circle.

2. Spread half the filling over the bottom layer of cake. Place middle layer on top of the filled bottom layer. Spread remaining filling over this layer and top with third layer, cut side down. Refrigerate until set, 15 to 20 minutes.

3. Make whipped cream frosting.

4. Frost the top and sides of the cakes with whipped cream frosting. Using a metal spatula, start at the top and continue to spread frosting down to cover cake sides. To garnish, sprinkle the top with chocolate chips.

5. Refrigerate until serving. Serve chilled.

YIELD: ONE 3-LAYER 10-INCH CAKE, ABOUT 25 SLICES

# SOUTH BEACH POPPYSEED CAKE

*This poppyseed cake accented with a fresh lime filling was inspired by the Florida sun. I usually bake one in winter and sip on an iced cappuccino to chase away the winter blues. The tart filling is the perfect partner to this poppyseed cake or a plain white cake.*

TWO 8-INCH LAYERS POPPYSEED CAKE (PAGE 65)

1 RECIPE LIME SEVEN-MINUTE FROSTING (PAGE 124)

1 RECIPE LIME FILLING (RECIPE FOLLOWS)

GARNISH: 1 TEASPOON POPPYSEEDS, GRATED LIME RIND

## LIME FILLING

¾ CUP SUGAR

2 TABLESPOONS CORNSTARCH

PINCH OF SALT

1 TABLESPOON GRATED LIME RIND

⅓ CUP LIME JUICE

½ CUP WATER

1 EGG, LIGHTLY BEATEN

1 TABLESPOON BUTTER

In a double boiler over simmering water, combine all ingredients. Cook, whisking constantly, until mixture thickens, 5 to 6 minutes. Remove from the heat. Cool. Cover with plastic wrap and refrigerate until ready to use.

**ASSEMBLY:**

1. Prepare all the ingredients.

2. Cut layers horizontally in half so you have 4 thin layers of cake. Place one layer cut side up on a cake plate or doily-covered cake circle. Using a pastry bag filled with frosting, pipe an outline of frosting along the outer edge of the layer. Spread a quarter of the chilled lime filing into frosting outline and over bottom layer of cake. Repeat the layering of cake and filling until cake is completed. Place top layer, cut side down, for final layer. The filling layers will be thin because they're very tart and rich.

3. Frost the outside of the cake with remaining frosting. Using a metal spatula start from the top and continue to spread on the sides of the cake. Lightly pull spatula away, creating small peaks. Garnish top with a sprinkle of grated lime rind and poppyseeds.

**4.** Refrigerate cake. Serve cake at room temperature.

YIELD: ONE 4-LAYER 8-INCH CAKE, 12 TO 15 SERVINGS

---

◆ **SERVE AT ROOM TEMPERATURE** ◆

MANY OF THESE CAKES NEED TO BE REFRIGERATED TO STAY FRESH. HOWEVER, MOST DO TASTE BETTER WHEN SERVED AT ROOM TEMPERATURE. REMOVE YOUR CAKE FROM THE REFRIGERATOR 1 TO 2 HOURS BEFORE SERVING SO THAT FROSTINGS CAN SOFTEN AND FLAVORS WILL BE AT THEIR PEAK.

---

# ICE BOX LAYER CAKE

*This layer cake version of the classic ice box cake combines a rich yellow butter cake, custard filling, sliced bananas, and graham cracker crumbs. A new classic! The custard makes a great filling for many classic layer cakes.*

TWO 9-INCH LAYERS YELLOW CAKE (PAGE 66)

1 RECIPE VANILLA CUSTARD FILLING (RECIPE FOLLOWS)

1 RECIPE WHIPPED CREAM FROSTING (PAGE 122)

1 LARGE BANANA, SLICED

1 CUP GRAHAM CRACKER CRUMBS

GARNISH: 1 BANANA, SLICED

## VANILLA CUSTARD FILLING

2 TABLESPOONS CORNSTARCH

PINCH OF SALT

⅓ CUP SUGAR

1 CUP HEAVY CREAM

3 EGGS

1 TABLESPOON BUTTER

1 TEASPOON VANILLA EXTRACT

1. In a double boiler over boiling water, combine cornstarch, salt, sugar, cream and eggs. Whisk constantly until mixture is thickened, about 5 minutes.

2. Remove from the heat. Stir in butter and vanilla. Cool. Cover with plastic and refrigerate.

ASSEMBLY:

1. Prepare all the ingredients.

2. Level off tops of yellow layer cakes. Place one layer, cut side up, on a serving plate or doily-covered cake circle. Using a pastry bag filled with about one-third of the whipped cream frosting, pipe an outline along the perimeter of the layer. Spoon and lightly spread the vanilla custard into the center of the cake. Arrange slices of banana in the custard.

3. Place the other layer, cut side down, on top of the bananas and custard. Press lightly. Frost the outside of the cake with remaining whipped cream, using a metal spatula and swirling motions. Start at the top and continue to spread frosting to cover sides. Don't worry if you have spots of cake showing through.

4. Place graham cracker crumbs in a flat plate. With one hand holding the cake underneath, use the other hand to cover the cake completely with crumbs. Hold the cake over the plate of crumbs so any excess will fall back into plate. Be sure to adhere crumbs while the frosting is fresh.

5. Refrigerate until serving. Just before serving, arrange banana slices on top of the cake. Serve chilled.

YIELD: ONE 2-LAYER 9-INCH CAKE, 12 TO 15 SERVINGS

---

◆ PASTRY TIPS ◆

THERE ARE MANY TYPES OF TIPS FOR PASTRY BAGS THAT ARE USED IN CAKE DECORATING. SOME OF THE MORE BASIC ONES TO ADD TO YOUR COLLECTION ARE: TIP #3, THE PERFECT WIDTH FOR WRITING ON CAKES AND MAKING POLKA DOTS; TIP #32 OR ANY OF THE OPEN STAR TIPS, WHICH ARE IDEAL FOR MAKING TOP AND BOTTOM BORDERS FOR YOUR CAKES. THE OPEN STAR TIPS ARE ALSO USED WHEN MAKING A DAM TO FILL LAYERS.

# AMARETTO APPLE CAKE

*This selection from our bakery menu is a Sweet Maria specialty. The baked apple filling is generously spiced with cinnamon and sugar, making this the perfect alternative to apple pie. (The filling is also a great dessert on its own, spooned over ice cream or pound cake.)*

TWO 9-INCH ROUND YELLOW CAKE
LAYERS (PAGE 66)

½ CUP AMARETTO LIQUEUR

1 RECIPE CREAM CHEESE FROSTING
(PAGE 122)

1 RECIPE APPLE FILLING (RECIPE
FOLLOWS)

2 CUPS SLICED ALMONDS, TOASTED

## APPLE FILLING

4 MEDIUM APPLES, PEELED, CORED,
AND CUT INTO ¼-INCH SLICES (ABOUT
4 CUPS)

½ CUP BROWN SUGAR

3 TEASPOONS CINNAMON

½ CUP WATER

Place apple slices in a small baking dish. Sprinkle with sugar and cinnamon. Pour water over apples and stir with a wooden spoon. Bake at 350°F for 20 to 25 minutes, or until apples are tender. Cool before using.

ASSEMBLY:

1. Prepare all the ingredients.

2. Level off the tops of yellow cake layers. Place one layer, cut side up, onto a serving plate or doily-covered cake circle. Using a pastry brush, brush the cake with about half the amaretto.

3. Spread a thin layer of cream cheese frosting on the cake. Using a pastry bag, pipe an outline along the outer edge of the layer. Spoon apple filling into center. Brush the cut side of other layer with remaining amaretto and place, cut side down, on top of apple filling. Press down lightly.

4. Frost the outside of the cake with remaining cream cheese frosting. Using a metal spatula, start at the top and continue to spread frosting covering the sides of the cake. Don't worry if the sides are imperfect and show crumbs. While the frosting is fresh, cover the sides and top with toasted almonds. Put the almonds on a flat

plate. Hold the cake underneath the plate with one hand. Use the other hand to adhere almonds to the sides of the cake. Hold the cake over the plate of almonds so any excess almonds will fall back onto the plate. Refrigerate. Serve cake at room temperature.

YIELD: ONE 2-LAYER 9-INCH CAKE, 12 TO 15 SERVINGS

# CHOCOLATE MANDARIN ORANGE CAKE

*This is our Devil's Food Cake, drizzled with Grand Marnier and filled with chocolate cream and mandarin oranges. The deep chocolate ganache coating makes it an ideal groom's cake. An old tradition, a groom's cake is usually a rich chocolate, and is often shaped into the symbol of a sport or hobby that the groom enjoys. Some recent ones that we've created are pool tables, tennis racquets, and grand pianos.*

TWO 9-INCH LAYERS DEVIL'S FOOD
CAKE (PAGE 67)

¼ CUP GRAND MARNIER

1 RECIPE CHOCOLATE BUTTERCREAM
(PAGE 120)

1 RECIPE CHOCOLATE GANACHE
(PAGE 123)

1 RECIPE CHOCOLATE CREAM FILLING
(RECIPE FOLLOWS)

2½ CUPS MANDARIN ORANGES

GARNISH: CHOCOLATE-DIPPED
MANDARIN ORANGES

## CHOCOLATE CREAM FILLING

2 CUPS HEAVY CREAM

½ CUP COCOA

½ CUP SUGAR

1. In an electric mixer with wire whip attachment, beat cream and cocoa on high speed until soft peaks form. Scrape down the sides of the bowl with a rubber spatula.

2. Add sugar and whip on high speed until stiff. Use immediately.

YIELD: 3 CUPS

ASSEMBLY:

1. Make chocolate buttercream. Set aside at room temperature in an airtight container or a bowl covered with plastic wrap.

2. Make chocolate ganache. Set aside to thicken.

3. Level off the tops of both layers of cake. Slice each layer in half horizontally to give you 4 thin layers. Place one layer, cut side up, on a 9-inch cake circle. Brush

with Grand Marnier. Using a pastry bag filled with chocolate buttercream, pipe an outline along the perimeter of the layer. Spoon and spread one-third of the chocolate cream filling into the center. Arrange one-third of the mandarin oranges on top of the chocolate cream. Place another cake layer on top of the filled layer.

4. Continue to brush and fill the layers until the cake is completely filled. Place top layer cut side down. Refrigerate the cake to set, 10 to 15 minutes.

5. Frost the outside of the cake with a thin layer of chocolate buttercream. Place the frosted cake on a wire rack. Place a clean sheet of parchment paper or waxed paper under the rack to catch any excess ganache. Carefully pour ganache over the top of the frosted cake. Use a metal spatula to help guide the ganache over the sides of the cake. Refrigerate cake.

6. When ganache is set or firm to the touch, adhere cake to serving plate or a doily-covered large cake circle.

7. Garnish with chocolate-dipped mandarin oranges. Refrigerate cake. Serve at room temperature.

YIELD: ONE 4-LAYER 9-INCH CAKE, 15 TO 18 SERVINGS

# HOLIDAY EGGNOG CAKE

*This cake has become a welcome addition to our family's traditional Italian Christmas Eve dessert buffet. The whipped cream, laced with cinnamon and nutmeg, is the perfect accent for this cake. Top it with fresh mint leaves and berries for a festive touch.*

1 CLASSIC SPONGE CAKE (BAKED IN A 10-INCH TUBE PAN (PAGE 34)

1 CUP RUM

2 RECIPES VANILLA CUSTARD FILLING (PAGE 72)

1 RECIPE SPICED WHIPPED CREAM FROSTING (RECIPE FOLLOWS)

GARNISH: FRESH MINT AND BERRIES

## SPICED WHIPPED CREAM FROSTING

2 CUPS HEAVY CREAM

¼ CUP SUGAR

1 TEASPOON CINNAMON

½ TEASPOON NUTMEG

In an electric mixer with wire whip attachment, beat cream until peaks form, about 2 minutes. Add sugar, cinnamon, and nutmeg and whip until stiff, about another 30 seconds. Use immediately.

ASSEMBLY:

1. Prepare all the ingredients except whipped cream.

2. Cut sponge cake into fourths, horizontally. Place the bottom layer, cut side up, on a serving dish or doily-covered cake circle. Sprinkle with ⅓ cup rum. Spread one-third of the vanilla custard onto cake. Place next layer on top of custard. Continue to fill the layers in the same manner. Place top layer cut side down.

3. Refrigerate the filled cake while making the whipped cream.

4. With a metal spatula, frost the top and sides of the cake with the spiced whipped cream. If desired, use a pastry bag to pipe a border along the top edge of the cake.

5. Refrigerate until serving. Garnish with fresh mint leaves and berries. Serve chilled.

YIELD: ONE 4-LAYER 10-INCH CAKE, ABOUT 25 SERVINGS

## ITALIAN RUM CAKE

Use plain white whipped cream to frost the cake instead of spiced whipped cream and cover the sides of the cake with sliced toasted almonds. Pipe a shell border around the top edge of the cake.

# TOASTED LEMON SNOWBALL CAKE

*Totally covered with toasted coconut, this white layer cake is filled with a flavor-packed lemon filling.*

TWO 8-INCH LAYERS WHITE CAKE
(PAGE 64)

1 RECIPE LEMON CURD FILLING
(RECIPE FOLLOWS)

1 RECIPE LEMON SEVEN-MINUTE
FROSTING (PAGE 124)

2 CUPS TOASTED COCONUT

GARNISH: GRATED LEMON RIND

## LEMON CURD FILLING

1 CUP SUGAR

1 TABLESPOON CORNSTARCH

5 EGG YOLKS

¼ CUP LEMON JUICE

1 TABLESPOON GRATED LEMON RIND

¼ POUND BUTTER

Place sugar and cornstarch in a medium saucepan. Stir until blended. Add egg yolks and whisk with a wire whisk until blended. Add lemon juice, rind, and butter. Whisk constantly over medium-low heat until thickened and bright yellow, 8 to 10 minutes. Do not boil. Cover with plastic wrap and refrigerate.

ASSEMBLY:

1. Prepare all the ingredients.

2. Level the tops of cakes. Place one layer, cut side up, on a serving plate or doily-covered cake circle. Using a pastry bag filled with frosting, pipe an outline of frosting around the perimeter of the layer. Spread the filling into outline and over cake layer. Place top layer, cut side down, on top of filled layer.

3. Frost the outside of the cake with remaining seven-minute frosting. Using a metal spatula, spread the icing starting at the top and spreading down around the sides. While the frosting is wet, cover the sides and top of cake with toasted coconut. Place coconut in a flat plate. Hold the cake underneath with one hand. Use the other hand to adhere coconut to the sides and top of cake. Hold the cake over the plate so that any excess coconut will fall back onto the plate. Be sure to adhere the coconut while the frosting is wet.

**4.** Refrigerate cake. Garnish with grated lemon rind. Serve at room temperature.

YIELD: ONE 2-LAYER 8-INCH CAKE, 10 TO 12 SERVINGS

---

♦ **L A Y E R S   O R   T I E R S** ♦

A LOT OF PEOPLE CONFUSE CAKE LAYERS WITH CAKE TIERS. TRY TO THINK OF LAYERS AS THE INTERIOR PART OF THE CAKE, THE PARTS OF THE CAKE THAT SANDWICH AND HOLD THE FILLINGS. TIERS ARE THE FINISHED FROSTED CAKES STACKED ONE ON TOP OF THE OTHER IN DESCENDING HEIGHT, LIKE A WEDDING CAKE.

---

# BLACK & TAN CAKE

*This cake combines our classic Yellow Layer Cake, mocha mousse filling, and a dark chocolate ganache coating. A rich indulgence for a special occasion, especially with a glass of champagne.*

TWO 9-INCH YELLOW CAKE LAYERS
(PAGE 66)

1 RECIPE CHOCOLATE BUTTERCREAM
(PAGE 121)

1 RECIPE MOCHA MOUSSE FILLING
(RECIPE FOLLOWS)

1 RECIPE CHOCOLATE GANACHE
(PAGE 123)

## MOCHA MOUSSE FILLING

2 CUPS HEAVY CREAM

3½ TABLESPOONS COCOA

1 TEASPOON INSTANT ESPRESSO

½ CUP SUGAR

Combine heavy cream, cocoa, espresso, and sugar. With an electric mixer with the wire whisk attachment, whip on high speed until soft peaks form, about 2 minutes. Scrape down the sides and bottom of the mixing bowl using a rubber spatula. This will ensure that your ingredients are well mixed. Continue whipping on high speed until stiff. Use immediately.

YIELD: 3 CUPS

ASSEMBLY:

1. Prepare all the ingredients except the ganache.

2. Level the tops of the cake layers. Cut layers horizontally in half to give you 4 thin layers. Place one layer, cut side up, on a serving plate or doily-covered cake circle. Using a pastry bag filled with chocolate buttercream, pipe an outline of frosting around the outer edge of the layer. Spread one-third of the mocha mousse filling into the outline. Place another layer on top of the filled layer. Continue to fill the layers in the same manner. Place the top layer cut side down. Refrigerate cake to set, 10 to 15 minutes.

3. Use a thin layer of chocolate buttercream frosting to coat the cake. Thin the frosting with water to help it spread. Using a metal spatula, start at the top and continue to spread frosting onto the sides of the cake. Set aside.

4. Prepare ganache.

5. Place frosted cake on a wire cooling rack with a clean piece of parchment or waxed paper underneath. Pour ganache over the top of the cake. Guide the glaze down the sides of the cake with a metal spatula. Smooth sides and top with a spatula. Refrigerate. Serve at room temperature.

YIELD: ONE 4-LAYER 9-INCH CAKE, 15 TO 18 SERVINGS

# TOASTED ALMOND CAKE

*This cake is bursting with almond flavor. It is great served alone or with a splash of Raspberry Sauce (page 58) poured over each piece. Enjoy it with a sip of a cordial, such as amaretto or Chambord.*

TWO 8-INCH LAYERS WHITE ALMOND
CAKE (PAGE 65)

1½ CUPS SLIVERED ALMONDS,
TOASTED

1 RECIPE ALMOND SEVEN-MINUTE
FROSTING (PAGE 124)

ASSEMBLY:

1. Make cake and frosting.

2. Level off the tops of both cake layers. Slice each layer in half horizontally to give you 4 thin layers. Place one layer, cut side up, on a serving plate or doily-covered cake circle.

3. Using a pastry bag filled with frosting, pipe an outline of frosting around the perimeter of the layer. Spread a thin layer of frosting inside the outline. Place another layer on top of frosting. Continue to layer until completely filled. Place the top layer cut side down.

4. Frost the outside of the cake with the remaining frosting. Start at the top and continue to spread frosting to cover the sides of the cake. Place almonds in a flat dish. With one hand holding the cake underneath, use the other hand to cover the cake with almonds. Hold the cake over the plate, letting the excess nuts fall back into the plate. Be sure to adhere almonds while the frosting is fresh.

5. Refrigerate. Serve at room temperature.

YIELD: ONE 4-LAYER 8-INCH CAKE, 12 TO 15 SERVINGS

# TURTLE CAKE

*This chocolate, caramel, and peanut concoction is based on the popular chocolate candy called "Turtles." It pairs our Devil's Food Cake with a gooey caramel center and peanuts. Make it for your favorite chocoholic's birthday.*

TWO 9-INCH LAYERS DEVIL'S FOOD
CAKE (PAGE 67)

1 RECIPE CHOCOLATE BUTTERCREAM
(PAGE 121)

½ CUP CARAMEL ICE CREAM TOPPING

½ CUP UNSALTED PEANUTS

GARNISH: 3 TABLESPOONS CARAMEL
TOPPING, PEANUTS

ASSEMBLY:

1. Make cake and buttercream frosting.

2. Level off the tops of cake layers. Place one layer, cut side up, on a serving plate or a doily-covered cake circle. Using a pastry bag filled with chocolate buttercream, pipe an outline of frosting around the perimeter of the layer. Spoon and spread the caramel topping into the center of the cake. Sprinkle peanuts on top of the caramel.

3. Place the other layer, cut side down, on top of the caramel. Refrigerate cake to set, 10 to 15 minutes.

4. Frost the outside of the cake with remaining chocolate buttercream, using a metal spatula to smooth. Start at the top of the cake and continue to spread to cover the sides. If desired, pipe a shell border along the edge of the top of the cake.

5. Using a fork, drizzle caramel in zigzags over the top of the cake. Sprinkle with peanuts. Refrigerate until serving. Serve at room temperature.

YIELD: ONE 2-LAYER 9-INCH CAKE, 12 TO 15 SERVINGS

# CRAN-RASPBERRY CAKE

*Meet someone special under the mistletoe with a piece of this cake and a glass of holiday eggnog. A favorite from our holiday selections, it has a tart fruit filling and a light whipped cream frosting.*

TWO 9-INCH YELLOW CAKE LAYERS
(PAGE 66)

1 RECIPE WHIPPED CREAM FROSTING
(PAGE 122)

1 RECIPE CRAN-RASPBERRY FILLING
(RECIPE FOLLOWS)

1½ CUPS TOASTED CHOPPED WALNUTS

GARNISH: CRANBERRIES AND RASP-
BERRIES

## CRAN-RASPBERRY FILLING

3 CUPS CRANBERRIES, FRESH OR
FROZEN

¼ CUP SUGAR

¼ CUP WATER

3 CUPS RASPBERRIES, FRESH OR
FROZEN

1. Rinse cranberries. Place in a small saucepan. Add sugar and water. Over medium heat, boil for 3 to 4 minutes, or until tender, stirring occasionally. Remove from the heat. Cool.

2. When cool, place in a medium mixing bowl. Stir in raspberries. Set aside.

ASSEMBLY:

1. Prepare all the ingredients.

2. Level the tops of two cake layers. Cut layers horizontally to give you 4 thin layers. Place one layer, cut side up, on a cake plate or doily-covered cake circle. Spread a thin layer of whipped cream over the cake. Using a pastry bag filled with whipped cream, pipe an outline around the outer edge of the layer. Fill the outline with one third of the filling. Repeat layering cake with filling until cake is filled. Place top layer cut side down.

3. Frost outside of cake with remaining whipped cream. Using a metal spatula, start at the top of the cake and continue to spread frosting onto the sides of the cake. Cover sides and top of cake with toasted walnuts. Place walnuts in a flat plate. Holding the cake from underneath with one hand, use the other hand to adhere nuts to top and sides of cake. Hold the cake over the plate of nuts so any excess

nuts will fall back onto the plate. Refrigerate cake. Garnish with fresh cranberries and raspberries. Refrigerate again. Serve chilled.

YIELD: ONE 4-LAYER 9-INCH CAKE, 15 TO 18 SERVINGS

# CONNECTICUT SPICE CAKE

*This flavorful cake pays tribute to my home state, also known as the Nutmeg State. It is a spiced version of our classic Yellow Layer Cake that is perfect for an autumn birthday cake or a non-pumpkin addition to your Thanksgiving desserts.*

TWO 9-INCH LAYERS SPICE CAKE

1 RECIPE CREAM CHEESE FROSTING
(PAGE 122)

GARNISH: SPRINKLE OF CINNAMON
AND NUTMEG

## SPICE CAKE

4 EGGS, SEPARATED

½ POUND BUTTER, SOFTENED

2 CUPS SUGAR

1 TEASPOON VANILLA EXTRACT

2½ CUPS CAKE FLOUR

2 TEASPOONS BAKING POWDER

¼ TEASPOON SALT

1½ TEASPOONS NUTMEG

3 TEASPOONS CINNAMON

1 TEASPOON GROUND CLOVES

1 CUP BUTTERMILK

1. Preheat oven to 350°F.

2. Grease and flour or line two 9-inch cake pans with parchment paper. Set aside.

3. In an electric mixer with wire whisk attachment, beat egg whites until stiff but not dry. Set aside.

4. In an electric mixer on medium speed, cream the butter. Gradually add the sugar and beat until light in color. Add vanilla. Add egg yolks, one at a time, beating well after adding each one.

5. In another bowl, combine flour, baking powder, salt, nutmeg, cinnamon, and cloves. Add to the egg yolk mixture alternately with the buttermilk. Begin and end with flour mixture. Mix until batter is smooth.

6. Carefully fold mixture into egg whites.

7. Pour batter into prepared pans. Bake for 25 to 30 minutes, or until a tester comes out with a fine crumb. Remove cakes from the oven. Cool cakes in pans on wire

cooling rack for 10 to 15 minutes. Remove cakes from the pans and continue to cool on wire racks. Remove and discard parchment.

YIELD: TWO 9-INCH CAKE LAYERS

ASSEMBLY:

1. Make the cake and cream cheese frosting.

2. Level the tops of the cakes. Place one layer, cut side up, on a serving plate or doily-covered cake circle. Spread a layer of frosting over cake. Place other layer, cut side down, on top.

3. Frost the outside of the cake, using the remaining cream cheese frosting. Using a metal spatula, start at the top of the cake and continue to spread to cover sides. Refrigerate cake. Sprinkle the top with cinnamon and nutmeg. Serve at room temperature.

YIELD: ONE 2-LAYER 9-INCH CAKE, 12 TO 15 SERVINGS

# THE ELVIS CAKE

*This chocolate, peanut butter, and banana combo was inspired by the King's favorite sandwich. I try to make one every January 8, Elvis's birthday.*

TWO 9-INCH LAYERS DEVIL'S FOOD
CAKE (PAGE 67)

1 RECIPE WHIPPED CREAM FROSTING
(PAGE 122)

1 CUP SMOOTH PEANUT BUTTER

1 LARGE BANANA

GARNISH: 1 TEASPOON PEANUT
BUTTER, 1 BANANA, SLICED, SPRINKLE
OF COCOA

ASSEMBLY:

1. Level off the tops of the two chocolate layers. Place one cake, cut side up, on a serving plate or doily-covered cake circle. Spread a thin layer of whipped cream over the layer. Drop spoonfuls of peanut butter on top of the thin cream layer. Slice banana and arrange in the center of the cake. Place the other layer, cut side down, on top of the peanut butter and bananas. Press gently.

2. Frost the cake with remaining whipped cream frosting, using a metal spatula with swirling strokes. Start at the top and continue to spread down the sides of the cake. Refrigerate cake. Top with a spoonful of peanut butter, slices of banana, and a dusting of cocoa. Serve chilled.

YIELD: ONE 2-LAYER 9-INCH CAKE, 12 TO 15 SERVINGS

# CRANBERRY PEAR CAKE

*This layer cake spotlights a tasty combination of pears, cranberries, and cinnamon. Try this perfect winter pick-me-up with a mug of hot mulled cider.*

TWO 9-INCH LAYERS YELLOW CAKE (PAGE 66)

1 RECIPE CREAM CHEESE FROSTING (PAGE 122)

1 RECIPE PEAR CRANBERRY FILLING (RECIPE FOLLOWS)

## PEAR CRANBERRY FILLING

4 BOSC PEARS, PEELED, CORED, AND SLICED (3 CUPS)

¼ CUP WATER

½ CUP SUGAR

1 CUP FRESH CRANBERRIES

Place sliced pears in a small baking dish. Stir in sugar and water. Bake at 350°F for 20 to 25 minutes, or until just beginning to get tender. Add cranberries to the pan. Continue baking for 10 to 15 minutes, or until tender. Cool before using.

ASSEMBLY:

1. Prepare all the ingredients.

2. Level off the tops of cake layers. Place one layer, cut side up, on a serving plate or doily-covered cake circle.

3. Spread a thin layer of cream cheese frosting on the cake. Using a pastry bag filled with cream cheese frosting, pipe an outline around the perimeter of the layer. Spoon and spread filling into the center. Reserve about ½ cup filling for the top of the cake. Place the other layer, cut side down, on top of the filling. Press down gently.

4. Frost the outside of the cake with remaining cream cheese frosting. Using a metal spatula, start at the top and continue to spread frosting covering the sides of the cake.

5. Spoon remaining filling in the center of the top of the cake. If desired, pipe a shell border around the filling. Refrigerate. Serve cake at room temperature.

YIELD: ONE 2-LAYER 9-INCH CAKE, 12 TO 15 SERVINGS

# TIRAMISÙ CAKE

*This cake is a great way to dress up the Classic Sponge Cake. It is a rich dessert based on the traditional Italian dessert that literally means "pick me up." Any type of coffee complements this cake, but a cup of espresso is definitely my favorite.*

1 RECIPE CLASSIC SPONGE CAKE
(BAKED IN 10-INCH TUBE PAN,
PAGE 34)

2 CUPS STRONGLY BREWED COFFEE
OR ESPRESSO, COOLED

1 RECIPE TIRAMISÙ FILLING (RECIPE
FOLLOWS)

3 TEASPOONS CINNAMON

1 RECIPE WHIPPED CREAM FROSTING
(PAGE 122)

GARNISH: CHOCOLATE SHAVINGS AND
A SPRINKLE OF CINNAMON

## TIRAMISÙ FILLING

1 CUP HEAVY CREAM

1 POUND MASCARPONE CHEESE,
SOFTENED

½ CUP SUGAR

2 TABLESPOONS COFFEE LIQUEUR

In an electric mixer with wire whisk attachment, whip heavy cream until stiff, 2 to 3 minutes. Add mascarpone cheese, sugar, and liqueur and mix until well blended. Use immediately or refrigerate in an airtight container.

**ASSEMBLY:**

1. Cut sponge cake into thirds, horizontally. Place the bottom layer, cut side up, onto serving dish or doily-covered cake circle. Pour coffee over all the cake layers to soak the sponge evenly.

2. Divide the filling into thirds. Spread one-third of the filling over coffee-soaked bottom layer. Sprinkle with 1 teaspoon of cinnamon. Repeat with other layer, placing the coffee-soaked layer carefully. Spread remaining filling on top of the layer. Sprinkle with cinnamon.

3. Chill filled cake while preparing whipped cream.

4. Using a metal spatula, frost the top and sides of the cake with whipped cream frosting. Start at the top and continue to spread to cover sides. If desired, use a pastry bag to pipe a border along the top of the cake.

5. Refrigerate. Garnish with chocolate shavings and a sprinkle of cinnamon. Serve chilled.

YIELD: ONE 3-LAYER 10-INCH CAKE, 20 TO 25 SERVINGS

---

◆ **W E D D I N G   C A K E S** ◆

THE TRADITION OF CAKES AT WEDDINGS BEGAN LONG AGO. THERE ARE MANY STORIES AND SUPERSTITIONS ABOUT EARLY WEDDING CAKES. IN MEDIEVAL TIMES, GUESTS WOULD BRING SMALL BREADS OR CAKES TO THE RECEPTION. THE WHEAT-BASED GIFTS WERE A SYMBOL OF FERTILITY FOR THE HAPPY COUPLE. THESE SMALL CAKES WERE STACKED ONE ON TOP OF THE OTHER, AND THE BRIDE AND GROOM WOULD KISS OVER THE TOP FOR GOOD LUCK. A FRENCH CHEF DECIDED TO FROST THE CAKES, AND THUS TIERED WEDDING CAKES WERE CREATED. TODAY, THE BRIDE AND GROOM CUT THEIR FIRST SLICE TO ENSURE THEIR HAPPINESS. IT WOULD BE BAD LUCK IF ANYONE ELSE WERE TO CUT IT.

# WHITE CHOCOLATE GANACHE WEDDING CAKE

*This two-tier wedding cake is a vision in swirled white chocolate. The 6-inch and 10-inch cakes are just right for an intimate celebration. It's not hard to make; just think of it as making two separate cakes. It helps to get organized and to be sure you have all the necessary ingredients and special supplies.*

*I love the natural and swirled look to this frosting. It looks quite striking adorned with fresh pansies. I always plant a good supply of various colors just in case a bride chooses this design.*

1½ RECIPES BUTTERCREAM FROSTING (PAGE 120)

1 RECIPE APRICOT CREAM FILLING (RECIPE FOLLOWS)

1 RECIPE WHITE CHOCOLATE GANACHE (RECIPE FOLLOWS)

GARNISH: FRESH FLOWERS (NONTOXIC, UNSPRAYED)

**SPECIAL SUPPLIES:**

6-INCH ROUND CAKE PAN, 3 INCHES DEEP

TWO 10-INCH ROUND CAKE PANS, 2 INCHES DEEP

ONE 6-INCH AND ONE 10-INCH ROUND FOAM CORE BOARDS

ONE 14-INCH ROUND ½-INCH-THICK PLYWOOD FOR BASE (OR STURDY CAKE PLATTER, IF NOT TRANSPORTING)

THREE ¼-INCH WOODEN DOWEL RODS CUT INTO 4 PIECES FOR BOTTOM TIER

SHEARS

HAMMER

## WHITE CAKE FOR WEDDING CAKE

*Please note: The following recipe doubles the White Layer Cake recipe on page 64. If you don't have a mixer large enough, mix the batter in two separate batches.*

5 CUPS CAKE FLOUR

3 CUPS SUGAR

6 TEASPOONS BAKING POWDER

1 TEASPOON SALT

½ POUND PLUS 5⅓ TABLESPOONS BUTTER

10 EGG WHITES

2 CUPS MILK

2 TEASPOONS VANILLA EXTRACT

1. Preheat oven to 350°F.

2. Grease and flour or line two 10-inch and one 6-inch cake pans with baking parchment. Set aside.

3. In an electric mixer on low speed, blend flour, sugar, baking powder, and salt until mixed. Add butter and mix until butter is uniformly blended.

4. In a separate bowl, mix egg whites, milk, and vanilla with a wire whisk.

5. Add egg mixture to flour mixture. Mix on medium speed for 2 minutes.

6. Scrape down the sides of the mixing bowl. Continue to beat on medium-high for 2 minutes, or until batter is blended and smooth.

7. Pour batter into prepared pans. Fill the 6-inch pan halfway. Then pour remaining batter evenly into the two 10-inch pans.

8. Bake for 30 to 35 minutes for 10-inch layers and an additional 5 to 6 minutes for 6-inch cake.

9. Remove cakes from the oven and cool in pans on wire rack 10 to 15 minutes. Remove cakes from the pans and continue to cool on wire racks. Remove and discard parchment.

## APRICOT CREAM FILLING

**2 CUPS HEAVY CREAM**                    **1 CUP APRICOT PRESERVES**

In an electric mixer with wire whisk attachment, beat cream until almost stiff. Add apricot preserves and whip until stiff. Use immediately.

## WHITE CHOCOLATE GANACHE

**1¾ POUND WHITE CHOCOLATE, FINELY CHOPPED**    **1¼ CUPS HEAVY CREAM**

Place finely chopped chocolate in a medium mixing bowl. Heat cream over medium heat until just boiling. Pour hot cream over chocolate and stir until smooth. Refrigerate for 15 to 20 minutes, or until thick enough to spread.

**ASSEMBLY** (see page 125):

1. Level off the tops of all the cake layers. Slice the 6-inch tier horizontally into 4 thin layers. Slice each of the 10-inch layers in half, to give you 4 thin layers.

2. Adhere one layer of the 6-inch cake onto a 6-inch foam core board. Using a pastry bag filled with buttercream frosting, pipe an outline around the outer edge of the layer. Spread a thin layer of apricot cream in the center. Place another layer on top of the filling. Repeat filling cake until complete. Place the top layer, cut side down, on the filling. Refrigerate.

3. Adhere a layer of 10-inch cake onto a 10-inch foam core board. Repeat the filling process the same as the 6-inch layer. Refrigerate both tiers for 10 to 15 minutes.

4. Frost both cakes with a thin layer of buttercream. Using a metal spatula, start from the top and continue to spread the frosting over the sides of the cake. It doesn't need to be totally smooth and perfect. Refrigerate cakes until set, 10 to 15 minutes.

5. When ganache is ready, place both cakes on a wire rack. Using a metal spatula in large swirling motions, spread the ganache. Start at the top and continue to spread and swirl over the sides. Reserve about ¾ cup of the ganache to touch up the cake after assembly. Refrigerate the cakes to set for 10 to 15 minutes.

6. Place bottom 10-inch tier on a sturdy plywood base, or a heavy tray. Use a 6-inch cake circle or cake pan to mark the area where the smaller tier will go. You can center the cake in the traditional manner or place it slightly off center. Use a toothpick or cake tester to trace the outline of the 6 inches in the appropriate spot.

7. Cut 3 dowel rods into 4 pieces ⅟₁₆ inch higher than the cake. Insert dowels, evenly spaced, into the interior of the outline. Carefully place the 6-inch cake onto the dowel rods. Sharpen the end of one longer dowel rod. Use a hammer to drive this dowel through the center of the 6-inch cake to the bottom base. This will secure your cake. Use shears to cut the top of the dowel even with the top of the cake.

8. Use the remaining ganache to cover any gaps between layers and to cover the dowel rod hole on top. Refrigerate cake until serving. Decorate as desired with a cascade of fresh flowers or fruit.

YIELD: 60 TO 65 WEDDING CAKE SLICES

## ◆ WEDDING CAKE TIPS ◆

### Transporting Your Wedding Cake

If you need to transport this wedding cake, try to find a cake box that measures the same size as the bottom base. If the base is 10-inches round, use a box that is 10-inches square. This way the cake will fit tightly with nowhere to move. Tear the cover off the box; you won't be able to use it. You can leave the cake uncovered or lightly cover it with a sheet of plastic wrap or cellophane. Place the box onto a towel positioned in a flat trunk or hatchback vehicle. *Do not place the cake on the seat of a car.* It needs to be flat. Be aware of the temperature. If you are traveling a long distance in the summer with a white chocolate coated cake, the trunk may become too hot. The ideal situation is an air-conditioned four-wheel drive vehicle or the floor of a van.

### Serving Your Wedding Cake

If you are cutting the wedding cake yourself, instead of having a caterer do it, unassemble the cake first. Place a metal spatula underneath the foam board of the top tier. Use both hands to grab underneath the cake and pull it off the dowel rods. Discard all dowel rods. Slice the cake as shown on page 101. For best results. Use a clean, long serrated knife. Clean the knife periodically and use a slow sawing motion.

### Planning and Preparing

If you decide to take on the responsibility of making a wedding cake, make it easy on yourself by doing a few tasks in advance. You can make your buttercream frosting in advance. And you can bake your layers in advance and freeze. Just be sure both cake and frosting are at room temperature before assembly.

### Decorating with Fresh Flowers

Fresh flowers are a beautiful and simple way to decorate cakes. But don't use toxic flowers or flowers sprayed with pesticide. Lightly rinse flowers under water and gently pat dry. If they are edible flowers, cut stems and place directly onto the cake in a desired fashion—either cascading down the front or grouped in small clusters around the cake. If the flowers are being used for decoration only, place a small amount of plastic wrap or clear cellophane underneath the flowers.

# CARROT BLUEBERRY CAKE

*This cake is easy to make and very flexible. You can substitute pineapple or raspberries for the blueberries, or make a more traditional carrot cake with raisins and walnuts. Either grate the carrots using a four-sided grater or chop them in a food processor. You can also use this recipe to make two loaf cakes.*

TWO 8-INCH LAYERS CARROT
BLUEBERRY CAKE

1 RECIPE CREAM CHEESE FROSTING
(PAGE 122)

GARNISH: GRATED CARROTS,
BLUEBERRIES, AND A SPRINKLE OF
CINNAMON

## CARROT BLUEBERRY CAKE

2 CUPS ALL-PURPOSE FLOUR

½ CUP SUGAR

1 CUP BROWN SUGAR

1¼ CUPS OIL

¼ CUP ORANGE JUICE

4 EGGS

2 TEASPOONS BAKING SODA

2 TEASPOONS CINNAMON

1 TEASPOON SALT

1 TEASPOON VANILLA EXTRACT

2 CUPS GRATED CARROTS

1 CUP FROZEN BLUEBERRIES, THAWED

1. Preheat oven to 350°F.

2. Grease and flour or line two 8-inch cake pans with parchment paper. Set aside.

3. In an electric mixer, combine all ingredients except carrots and blueberries. Beat until well blended, about 2 minutes on medium speed. Scrape down the sides and bottom of the bowl to be sure all ingredients are incorporated. Beat until light in color, 2 to 3 minutes.

4. Stir in carrots and blueberries. Pour batter into prepared pans.

5. Bake for 35 to 40 minutes, or until a tester comes out with a fine crumb. Remove pans from the oven. Cool cakes in pans on wire cooling racks for 10 to 15 minutes. Carefully remove cakes from the pans and continue to cool on wire cooling racks. Remove and discard parchment.

ASSEMBLY:

1. Make cake and cream cheese frosting.

2. Level off tops of cake layers. Place one layer, cut side up, on a cake plate or doily-covered cake circle. Spread a layer of frosting over the cake layer. Place other layer, cut side down, onto bottom layer. Using a metal spatula, frost the outside of the cake with remaining cream cheese frosting. Start at the top and continue to spread frosting onto the sides of the cake. Refrigerate cake. Garnish with grated carrots, blueberries, and a sprinkle of cinnamon. Serve at room temperature.

YIELD: ONE 2-LAYER 8-INCH CAKE, 10 TO 12 SERVINGS

VARIATIONS:

## CARROT RASPBERRY CAKE
Substitute 1 cup frozen raspberries for the blueberries.

## TRADITIONAL CARROT CAKE
Omit frozen blueberries. Add ¾ cup walnut halves, ½ cup raisins, and ¼ cup chocolate chips in step 4.

## LOAF CAKES
Pour batter into two 8 x 4 x 3-inch loaf pans. Bake for 50 to 55 minutes.

◆  F I R S T   B I R T H D A Y S  ◆

FOR A CHILD'S FIRST BIRTHDAY, MANY PEOPLE ORDER A SMALL 6-INCH ROUND CAKE FOR THE GUEST OF HONOR ALONG WITH A LARGER CAKE FOR THE REST OF THE GUESTS. THIS SMALL CAKE IS FOR THE ONE-YEAR-OLD TO HAVE ALL TO HIMSELF, TO EAT, TO PLAY WITH, OR TO JUST MAKE A MESS.

# BANANA SOUR CREAM CAKE

*This banana cake is accented by rich chocolate buttercream frosting. It is exceptionally moist and tastes great for days. You can add walnuts if you'd like a traditional banana nut cake. Try a slice with an ice cold glass of milk.*

TWO 9-INCH BANANA SOUR CREAM
CAKE LAYERS

1 RECIPE CHOCOLATE BUTTERCREAM
(PAGE 121)

GARNISH: 1 BANANA, SLICED

## BANANA SOUR CREAM CAKE

¼ POUND BUTTER, SOFTENED

1 CUP SUGAR

½ CUP BROWN SUGAR

1 TEASPOON VANILLA EXTRACT

3 EGGS

2 CUPS CAKE FLOUR

1 TEASPOON BAKING POWDER

1 TEASPOON BAKING SODA

½ TEASPOON SALT

¾ CUP SOUR CREAM

2 CUPS MASHED BANANAS (2 TO 3
MEDIUM BANANAS)

1. Preheat oven to 350°F.

2. Grease and flour or line two 9-inch cake pans with parchment paper. Set aside.

3. In an electric mixer on medium speed, cream the butter. Gradually add sugar and brown sugar and mix until light. Add vanilla. Add eggs, one at a time, beating well after each one.

4. In a medium bowl, combine flour, baking powder, baking soda, and salt. In another small bowl, combine sour cream and mashed bananas. Pour each of these mixtures alternately into the butter mixture. Begin and end with flour mixture. Mix until blended.

5. Pour batter evenly into prepared pans. Bake for 20 to 25 minutes, or until a tester comes out with a fine crumb.

6. Remove pans from the oven and place on wire cooling racks. Cool in pans for 10 to 15 minutes. Carefully remove cakes from the pans and continue to cool on wire racks. Remove and discard parchment. Cool completely.

1. Make cake and chocolate buttercream.

2. Level off the tops of cake layers. Place one layer, cut side up, on a serving plate or doily-covered cake circle. Spread a layer of frosting onto the cake layer. Place other layer, cut side down, on top of the bottom layer. Frost the cake with remaining frosting.

3. Using a metal spatula, start at the top and continue to spread frosting onto the sides of the cake. Refrigerate. Garnish with sliced banana before serving. Serve at room temperature.

YIELD: ONE 2-LAYER 9-INCH CAKE, 12 TO 15 SERVINGS

---

◆ **HOW TO SERVE A LAYER CAKE** ◆

YOU CAN CUT A FILLED LAYER CAKE SEVERAL DIFFERENT WAYS. THE MOST IMPORTANT THING IS TO USE A CLEAN, SHARP, SERRATED KNIFE, AND TO USE A SAWING MOTION. ALSO, TAKE YOUR TIME. IF YOU'RE IN A HURRY, YOU MIGHT SMASH OR CRUMBLE THE SLICE. AFTER CUTTING, CAREFULLY USE A FORK OR PIE SERVER TO TRANSFER THE SLICE TO A DISH.

YOU CAN CUT SMALL CAKES INTO WEDGES, SIMILAR TO CUTTING PIZZA. OR YOU CAN CUT A STRIP HORIZONTALLY, AND THEN CUT SLICES FROM THE STRIP. THIS METHOD WORKS ESPECIALLY WELL WITH A LARGER CAKE.

---

# VERY BERRY
# WHIPPED CREAM CAKE

*Accented by fresh fruit, this cake is our most popular whipped cream cake. It's especially popular for Fourth of July parties. Not only is it a great, refreshing summer dessert, it proudly displays our red, white, and blue.*

TWO 8-INCH WHITE CAKE LAYERS
(PAGE 64)

1 RECIPE WHIPPED CREAM FROSTING
(PAGE 122)

1 CUP FRESH OR FROZEN
BLUEBERRIES

1 CUP FRESH OR FROZEN
RASPBERRIES

1 CUP FRESH STRAWBERRIES,
CLEANED, HULLED, AND SLICED

ASSEMBLY:

1. Make cake and whipped cream frosting.

2. Mix all berries together in a small bowl. Set aside.

3. Level the tops of the cakes. Slice both layers of cake in half horizontally, giving you 4 thin layers. Place one piece of cake, cut side up, on a serving plate or doily-covered cake circle. Spread a thin layer of whipped cream on the layer. Arrange one-third of the berry mixture over the cream. Repeat spreading cream and arranging berries until the cake is completely filled. Place top layer cut side down.

4. Using a metal spatula, frost the top and sides of the cake with remaining whipped cream. Garnish with berries.

5. Refrigerate until serving. Serve chilled.

YIELD: ONE 4-LAYER 8-INCH CAKE, 15 TO 18 SERVINGS

# FROZEN ALMOND
# STRAWBERRY CAKE

*Use our classic Almond Pound Cake to create this frozen dessert. It's a great make-ahead dessert—you can leave it in the freezer for up to 2 months and have a fabulous dessert for unexpected guests.*

1 ALMOND POUND CAKE (PAGE 18)

1 QUART STRAWBERRY ICE CREAM, SLIGHTLY SOFTENED

1 CUP CLEANED, HULLED, AND SLICED STRAWBERRIES

2 TABLESPOONS AMARETTO LIQUEUR

½ CUP SUGAR

½ CUP HEAVY CREAM

½ CUP SLICED ALMONDS

CONFECTIONERS' SUGAR FOR DUSTING

1. Line a large loaf pan (10 x 6 x 2½ inches) with plastic wrap. Leave enough wrap to cover loaf pan.

2. Cut pound cake lengthwise into 6 pieces. Line the prepared pan with slices of cake—one slice on the bottom, one slice on each long side of the pan. Split one slice to line the short ends of the pans.

3. In a large mixing bowl, quickly combine ice cream, strawberries, amaretto, sugar, heavy cream, and almonds. Stir with a wooden spoon until blended.

4. Spread half the ice cream mixture into the pan. Cover with a slice of cake. Spread remaining ice cream mixture on top of the cake and place the last slice of cake on top. Cover well with plastic wrap.

5. Freeze for 4 to 5 hours or overnight.

6. Thaw slightly before serving. Dust with confectioners' sugar. Using a sharp knife, slice into ½-inch pieces.

YIELD: ONE LARGE FILLED LOAF, ABOUT 12 SERVINGS

# GINGERBREAD

*This cake is so tasty you won't want to wait for Christmas to make it. It really does work year-round—I've even done a wedding cake in April with gingerbread. (It was a very traditional three-tier round cake with simple frosting draping, or swags, around the sides, and topped with a cluster of pale pink frosting roses.)*

*This cake is very flexible and tastes great with either Cream Cheese Frosting or Spiced Whipped Cream Frosting. To garnish the cake, use gingersnap crumbs to cover the cake, a sprinkle of orange rind, and cinnamon.*

TWO 8-INCH GINGERBREAD CAKE
LAYERS

1 RECIPE CREAM CHEESE FROSTING
(PAGE 122)

OR

1 RECIPE SPICED WHIPPED CREAM
FROSTING (PAGE 78)

1 CUP GINGERSNAP CRUMBS

GARNISH: GRATED ORANGE RIND AND A
SPRINKLE OF CINNAMON

## GINGERBREAD CAKE

12 TABLESPOONS BUTTER, MELTED

1 CUP MOLASSES

1 CUP BROWN SUGAR

1½ CUPS BUTTERMILK

3 EGGS

3 CUPS UNBLEACHED FLOUR

1 TEASPOON BAKING SODA

¼ TEASPOON SALT

3 TEASPOONS GROUND GINGER

1½ TEASPOONS CINNAMON

½ TEASPOON NUTMEG

1. Preheat oven to 350°F. Grease and flour or line two 8-inch cake pans with parchment paper.

2. In an electric mixer on medium speed, beat butter, molasses, brown sugar, buttermilk, and eggs.

3. Add dry ingredients and mix just until blended. Batter will be slightly lumpy. Do not overmix. Pour batter evenly into prepared pans. Bake for 30 to 35 minutes, or until a tester comes out with a fine crumb. Remove pans from the oven. Let cakes cool in pans on wire cooling racks for 10 to 15 minutes. Carefully re-

move cakes from the pans and turn bottom side down on racks to cool. Remove and discard parchment.

**ASSEMBLY:**

1.  Make cake and whipped cream or cream cheese frosting.

2.  Level off the tops of cake layers. Place one layer, cut side up, on a cake plate or doily-covered cake circle. Spread some frosting on the bottom layer. Place other layer, cut side down, onto bottom layer.

3.  Using a metal spatula, frost the outside of the cake with remaining frosting. Start from the top and continue to spread frosting onto the sides of the cake. Cover cake with crushed gingersnap crumbs. Place crumbs onto a flat plate. Hold the cake underneath with one hand. Use the other hand to adhere crumbs to the sides and top of the cake. Be sure to hold the cake over the plate of crumbs so that excess crumbs will fall back onto plate. Refrigerate cake. Garnish with grated orange rind and a sprinkle of cinnamon. Serve cake at room temperature.

YIELD: ONE 2-LAYER 8-INCH CAKE, 10 TO 12 SERVINGS

# CHIP & ERNIE'S CAKE

*This is a favorite from the Sweet Maria's menu. It's especially popular for children's birthday parties. A variation of our Yellow Layer Cake, it is made with chocolate chips and a rich chocolate icing. Be sure to line the cake pan with parchment. This will prevent the chocolate chips from sticking to the pan.*

TWO 9-INCH CHOCOLATE CHIP CAKE LAYERS

1 RECIPE CHOCOLATE BUTTERCREAM (PAGE 121)

GARNISH: CHOCOLATE CHIPS

## CHOCOLATE CHIP CAKE

4 EGGS, SEPARATED

½ POUND BUTTER, SOFTENED

1 CUP SUGAR

1 CUP BROWN SUGAR

1 TEASPOON VANILLA EXTRACT

2½ CUPS ALL-PURPOSE FLOUR

2 TEASPOONS BAKING POWDER

¼ TEASPOON SALT

1 CUP BUTTERMILK

1½ CUPS SEMISWEET CHOCOLATE CHIPS

1. Preheat oven to 350°F.

2. Grease and line two 9-inch cake pans with parchment paper. Set aside.

3. In an electric mixer with wire whisk attachment, beat egg whites until stiff but not dry. Set aside.

4. In an electric mixer on medium speed, cream the butter. Gradually add the sugar and brown sugar and beat until light. Add vanilla. Add egg yolks, one at a time, beating well after each egg.

5. Combine flour, baking powder, and salt. Add to the butter mixture alternately with buttermilk. Begin and end with the flour mixture. Mix just until blended. Fold egg whites into flour mixture. Fold in chocolate chips.

6. Pour batter into prepared pans. Bake for 25 to 30 minutes, or until a tester comes out with a fine crumb.

7.  Remove pan from the oven and place on wire cooling rack. Cool cakes in pans for 8 to 10 minutes. Carefully remove cakes from the pans and continue to cool on wire rack. Remove and discard parchment.

**ASSEMBLY:**

1.  Make cake and chocolate buttercream.

2.  Level tops of baked layers. Adhere one layer to a cake plate or doily-covered cake circle, cut side up. Spread some frosting in the center of the layer. Place the other layer on top, cut side down.

3.  Starting at the top, frost top of cake with metal spatula, using large swirling motions. Continue to frost sides, covering the entire cake. Use a little of water to help to thin and spread the frosting. Refrigerate cake. Garnish with chocolate chips. Serve at room temperature.

**YIELD: ONE 2-LAYER 9-INCH CAKE, 12 TO 15 SERVINGS**

# RUM RAISIN BANANA TRIFLE

*If you're still intimidated by assembling and decorating a layer cake, use this traditional dessert to have your cake and eat it too. It's the ideal solution to broken cakes—it can be made from any thin layers accumulated from leveling off the tops of cake layers, no matter what flavor. I try to recycle these "scraps" for a casual family dessert I call "cake in a bowl."*

FOUR 8- OR 9-INCH PIECES OF CAKE, ANY FLAVOR, SLICED VERY THIN

½ CUP DARK RUM

ONE RECIPE VANILLA CUSTARD FILLING (PAGE 72)

4 BANANAS, SLICED

1 CUP RAISINS

1 CUP LARGE WALNUT PIECES

ONE RECIPE CHOCOLATE CREAM FILLING (PAGE 76)

ONE RECIPE WHIPPED CREAM FROSTING (PAGE 122)

**ASSEMBLY:**

1. Place one layer of cake in a 3-quart trifle bowl. Drizzle the cake layer with rum. Spread half of the vanilla custard over the cake layer. Arrange bananas, raisins, and nuts over the top. Continue layering, alternating chocolate and vanilla filling, until the trifle bowl is filled. Spread whipped cream on top. If desired, pipe a design with a star tip on top. Garnish with raisins and walnut halves.

2. Refrigerate until serving. Serve chilled.

YIELD: 15 TO 18 SERVINGS

**VARIATIONS:**

If you have less cake than 4 pieces, use a smaller bowl and only one type of custard filling.

You can substitute any type of cake, custard, liqueur, fruit, or nuts you happen to have in your kitchen.

# LEMON RASPBERRY WHIPPED CREAM CAKE

*This popular cake combines two of my favorite flavors. It started as a "cake of the month" and soon became part of our regular menu.*
*It's perfect for a bridal luncheon or tea.*

TWO 8-INCH LAYERS WHITE LAYER
CAKE (PAGE 64)

1 RECIPE LEMON DRIZZLE (RECIPE
FOLLOWS)

1 RECIPE WHIPPED CREAM FROSTING
(PAGE 122)

3 CUPS FRESH OR INDIVIDUALLY
QUICK-FROZEN (IQF) RASPBERRIES

GARNISH: RASPBERRIES AND GRATED
LEMON RIND

## LEMON DRIZZLE

¼ CUP WATER

2 TABLESPOONS LEMON EXTRACT

Mix together in a small cup.

**ASSEMBLY:**

1. Prepare all the ingredients.

2. Level the tops of the cakes. Slice both cake layers in half horizontally, giving you 4 thin layers. Place one piece of cake, cut side up, on a serving plate or doily-covered cake circle. Using a pastry brush, brush the cake with lemon drizzle. Spread a thin layer of whipped cream frosting on the layer. Arrange 1 cup of berries over the cream. Place another layer on top of the berries. Repeat brushing, spreading whipped cream, and arranging berries until the cake is completely filled. Place the last layer cut side down.

3. Using a metal spatula, frost the top and sides of cake with remaining whipped cream. Garnish with raspberries and lemon rind.

4. Refrigerate until serving. Serve chilled.

YIELD: ONE 4-LAYER 8-INCH CAKE, 15 TO 18 SERVINGS

# JOSEPHINE & NAPOLEON CAKE

*This cake has a unique combination of sponge cake and puff pastry—the flaky dough
that is the basis for the napoleon pastry—and a combination of vanilla and chocolate
custard fillings. It may seem like a lot of steps, but it's well worth the effort.
The best way to approach it is to bake your sponge cake first. While it's in the oven,
make the custards and refrigerate them. Then make the puff pastry circles.
Assemble later, or the next day.*

½ RECIPE SPONGE CAKE

2 RECIPES VANILLA CUSTARD FILLING
(PAGE 72)

1 RECIPE CHOCOLATE CUSTARD
FILLING (RECIPE FOLLOWS)

TWO 10-INCH CIRCLES OF PUFF
PASTRY, BAKED (RECIPE FOLLOWS)

CONFECTIONERS' SUGAR FOR DUSTING

## TO MAKE HALF THE SPONGE CAKE

*Be aware that the cake will come only halfway up the sides of the pan and that the
cooking time will be a little less than the full recipe.*

4 EGG WHITES

½ CUP PLUS 2 TABLESPOONS SUGAR

¼ TEASPOON CREAM OF TARTAR

¼ TEASPOON SALT

4 EGG YOLKS

½ TEASPOON VANILLA EXTRACT

¾ CUP CAKE FLOUR

2 TABLESPOONS COLD WATER

1. Preheat oven to 325°F.

2. In an electric mixer with wire whisk attachment, beat egg whites, 2 tablespoons
   of sugar, cream of tartar, and salt. Start on medium speed, then use high speed
   until very stiff peaks form, 3 to 4 minutes. Set aside.

3. In a separate bowl, with an electric mixer on medium speed, beat the egg yolks,
   ½ cup of sugar, and vanilla. Beat until light in color, 2 to 3 minutes.

4. Alternate adding flour and water to egg yolk mixture. Begin and end with flour.
   Mix just until blended.

5. Using a rubber spatula, fold egg yolk mixture into beaten whites. When blended, spoon batter into a 10-inch ungreased tube pan with removable bottom.

6. Bake for 30 minutes, or until top is golden brown. Remove pan from the oven. Invert cake and cool in pan for about 1 hour.

7. When cool, carefully remove the cake from the pan. Use a sharp straight knife to loosen the outside of the cake from the pan. Remove inside of pan. Run knife along the bottom and around inside of center column to remove.

## CHOCOLATE CUSTARD FILLING

| | |
|---|---|
| 2 TABLESPOONS CORNSTARCH | 3 EGGS |
| PINCH OF SALT | 3 TABLESPOONS COCOA |
| ⅓ CUP SUGAR | 1 TABLESPOON BUTTER |
| 1 CUP HEAVY CREAM | 1 TEASPOON VANILLA EXTRACT |

1. In a double boiler over boiling water, combine cornstarch, salt, sugar, cream, eggs, and cocoa. Whisk constantly until mixture is thickened, about 5 minutes.

2. Remove from the heat. Stir in butter and vanilla. Cool. Cover with plastic wrap and refrigerate.

**TO MAKE PUFF PASTRY CIRCLES:**

1 PACKAGE (2 SHEETS) FROZEN PUFF PASTRY

1. Preheat oven to 375°F.

2. Follow the directions on the box and thaw slightly. Carefully unroll the sheets. Cut both sheets into two 10-inch circles. Make a hole, about 2 inches in diameter, in the center, using a cookie cutter. This will line up with the center hole in your sponge cake when you assemble the layers.

3. Place each circle separately onto a parchment-lined cookie sheet. Bake until lightly browned, 12 to 15 minutes.

4. Cool on cookie sheet.

5. Insteaad of discarding unused portions of puff pastry, sprinkle unused portions with cinnamon and sugar and bake. These are great snacks.

1. Slice the sponge cake in half horizontally. Place the bottom layer, cut side up, on a cake plate or doily-covered cake circle. Spread half the vanilla custard over sponge cake layer. Top with a circle of baked puff pastry. Spread the chocolate custard on top of the puff pastry. Top with the sponge cake layer. Repeat spreading another layer of vanilla custard and top with the last layer of puff pastry.

2. Refrigerate until serving. Dust with confectioners' sugar just before serving. Serve chilled. Use a sharp serrated knife with a slow sawing motion to cut cake into slices.

YIELD: ONE 4-LAYER 10-INCH CAKE, ABOUT 25 SERVINGS

# PIÑA COLADA CAKE

*This pineapple, rum, and coconut cake is very popular at Sweet Maria's.*
*People order it for special occasions or for an everyday dessert.*
*(We sometimes call it "the Booze Cruise.")*

TWO 9-INCH YELLOW CAKE LAYERS
(PAGE 66)

½ CUP RUM

1 RECIPE WHIPPED CREAM FROSTING
(PAGE 122)

3 CUPS CRUSHED PINEAPPLE, DRAINED

2 CUPS SHREDDED COCONUT

ASSEMBLY:

1. Make cake and whipped cream frosting.

2. Level off the tops of cake layers. Slice each layer in half horizontally to give you 4 thin layers. Place one layer, cut side up, on a serving plate or doily-covered cake circle. Using a pastry brush, brush the layer with rum. Spread a thin layer of whipped cream frosting over the cake. Using a pastry bag filled with whipped cream frosting, pipe an outline around the edge of the layer. Fill in the layer with 1 cup crushed pineapple. Place another layer on top of the filling. Repeat brushing with rum and filling all layers until cake is filled. Place top layer cut side down.

3. Frost the outside of the cake using the remaining whipped cream frosting. Start at the top and continue to spread to cover sides.

4. Place coconut in a flat plate. With one hand holding the cake underneath, use the other hand to adhere coconut to the top and sides of cake. Hold the cake over the plate. Let any excess coconut fall back onto the plate. Refrigerate until serving. Serve chilled.

YIELD: ONE 4-LAYER 9-INCH CAKE, 15 TO 18 SERVINGS

# LESS-FAT MOCHA CAKE

*This cake uses a chocolate angel food cake as its base. It is accented by a tasty mocha filling that actually tastes better the day after it's assembled. Fill the center hole with fresh berries or grapes to garnish your dessert. Enjoy with a glass of sparkling cider.*

ONE 10-INCH CHOCOLATE ALMOND
ANGEL FOOD CAKE (PAGE 37)

1 RECIPE LOW-FAT MOCHA FILLING
(RECIPE FOLLOWS)

CONFECTIONERS' SUGAR FOR DUSTING

GARNISH: ASSORTED GRAPES OR
BERRIES

## LOW-FAT MOCHA FILLING

1 POUND NEUFCHÂTEL CHEESE,
SOFTENED

2 TEASPOONS INSTANT COFFEE

1 TEASPOON ALMOND EXTRACT

2 TABLESPOONS COCOA

½ CUP CONFECTIONERS' SUGAR

In an electric mixer on medium-high speed, whip cheese until light and fluffy, 3 to 5 minutes. Add coffee, almond extract, and cocoa. Beat until blended. Add confectioners' sugar and beat until blended. Use immediately or refrigerate in an airtight container overnight.

**ASSEMBLY:**

1. Slice angel food cake horizontally into 3 pieces. Place bottom layer, cut side up, on a cake plate or doily-covered cake circle. Spread half the mocha filling over the cake layer. Top with next layer of cake. Spread remaining filling on top of this layer. Top with last layer of cake, cut side down. Chill until serving.

2. Before serving, dust with confectioners' sugar and garnish with berries and/or grapes in the center and around cake. Serve chilled.

YIELD: ONE 3-LAYER 10-INCH CAKE, 18 TO 20 SERVINGS

# BROWN DERBY CAKE

*This cake was a specialty of the first bakery I worked in. It's a mound of delicious chocolate cake, filled with fresh strawberries and bananas and topped with whipped cream. It is fun to frost because you use your hands to spread the cream into a rounded top.*

TWO 9-INCH DEVIL'S FOOD CAKE LAYERS (PAGE 67)

1 RECIPE WHIPPED CREAM FROSTING (RECIPE FOLLOWS)

2 BANANAS SLICED

2 CUPS WASHED, HULLED, AND SLICED FRESH STRAWBERRIES

CHOCOLATE CAKE CRUMBS (MADE FROM EXTRA LAYER)

## WHIPPED CREAM FROSTING FOR DERBY CAKE

3 CUPS HEAVY CREAM

½ CUP SUGAR

In an electric mixer with wire whisk attachment, whip cream on high speed until peaks form, about 2 minutes. Add sugar. Continue to whip until stiff, another 30 seconds. Use immediately.

ASSEMBLY:

1. Cut cake layers in half horizontally so that you have 4 thin layers. Place one layer, cut side up, on a 9-inch cake circle. A circle will work easier for handling than a cake plate. Spread a thin layer of whipped cream frosting over the cake. Slice a banana in half lengthwise and place along the outer edge of the layer. Fill the center with half of the sliced strawberries. Top with another layer of chocolate cake. Repeat, spreading whipped cream, placing banana around the edge, and filling the center with remaining strawberries. Top with the third layer of cake. Chill.

2. With remaining cake layer, make crumbs: Rub the cake layer onto a grater, creating chocolate cake crumbs. Place crumbs in a pie plate or flat dish.

3. Remove chilled cake from the refrigerator. Holding the cake underneath with one hand, spread a large rounded mound of whipped cream on top of the cake with the other hand. Spread cream to cover layers and create a mound on top. Still holding the cake from the bottom, evenly spread cake crumbs all over mound to cover. Some of the white cream will show through.

4. Place the cake on a cake plate or larger doily-covered cake circle.

5. Refrigerate until serving. Serve chilled.

YIELD: ONE 3-LAYER 9-INCH CAKE, 15 TO 20 SERVINGS

# HAZELNUT CAKE

*This cake is a nut-lover's dream come true. In this versatile recipe you can use any type of nut you prefer: almonds or hazelnuts, or a combination of both, work great. Filled with a rich chocolate ganache and raspberry preserves and frosted with a hazelnut buttercream, it's so rich it should be eaten one sliver at a time.*

TWO 8-INCH ROUND LAYERS HAZELNUT CAKE

GANACHE FILLING (RECIPE FOLLOWS)

1 RECIPE HAZELNUT BUTTERCREAM (RECIPE FOLLOWS)

¼ CUP RASPBERRY PRESERVES

GARNISH: FRESH RASPBERRIES, HAZELNUTS, AND MINT LEAVES

## HAZELNUT CAKE

3 EGGS

2 CUPS SUGAR

1 CUP VEGETABLE OIL

1 CUP MILK

3 TEASPOONS HAZELNUT LIQUEUR

2 CUPS CAKE FLOUR

1 TEASPOON BAKING POWDER

¼ CUP HAZELNUTS, FINELY CHOPPED

1.  Preheat oven to 350°F. Grease and flour or line two 8-inch round cake pans with parchment paper.

2.  In an electric mixer, blend eggs, sugar, oil, milk, and liqueur. Add flour and baking powder. Mix until smooth. Stir in nuts.

3.  Pour batter evenly into prepared pans. Bake for 25 to 30 minutes, or until a tester comes out with a fine crumb. Remove pans from the oven. Cool cakes in pans on wire racks for 10 to 15 minutes.

4.  Carefully remove cakes from pans and set on wire cooling racks to cool completely. Remove and discard parchment.

## GANACHE FILLING

4 OUNCES FINELY CHOPPED SEMISWEET CHOCOLATE

¼ CUP HEAVY CREAM

1.  Place finely chopped chocolate in a small bowl.

2. In a small saucepan over medium-low heat, heat cream until just about boiling. Remove from the stove and pour over chocolate. Stir until well blended and smooth. Let cool at room temperature, then chill until thickened, the consistency of pudding.

## HAZELNUT BUTTERCREAM

½ POUND BUTTER, SOFTENED

6 CUPS CONFECTIONERS' SUGAR

1 TEASPOON VANILLA EXTRACT

¼ CUP HAZELNUTS, FINELY CHOPPED

2 EGG WHITES

1. In an electric mixer on low speed, cream the butter with 4 cups of confectioners' sugar. Add vanilla. Gradually add remaining 2 cups of confectioners' sugar, hazelnuts, and egg whites. Beat on high speed until light in color and texture, about 5 minutes.

2. Use immediately or place in an airtight container and refrigerate. Bring frosting to room temperature before using. Thin with a few teaspoons of water for easy spreading.

**ASSEMBLY:**

1. Slice hazelnut layers in half horizontally, to give you 4 thin layers of cake. Place one layer, cut side up, on a cake plate or doily-covered cake circle. Using hazelnut buttercream, pipe a dam around the outer edge of the layer. Fill the dam with half the ganache. Top with another layer of cake. Make a dam along the outer edge of the layer. Fill this dam with raspberry preserves. Top with another layer of cake. Pipe a buttercream dam along the edge of the layer. Fill this dam with remaining ganache. Top the cake with the last layer of cake, cut side down. Press lightly and refrigerate until set, 15 to 20 minutes.

2. Frost the outside of the cake with hazelnut buttercream. Using a metal spatula, start at the top and continue to spread frosting to cover the sides of the cake. Refrigerate cake. Garnish with fresh raspberries, hazelnuts, and mint leaves. Serve cake at room temperature.

**YIELD: ONE 4-LAYER 8-INCH CAKE, 12 TO 15 SERVINGS**

# CHOCOLATE CREAM–FILLED CUPCAKES AND LEMON CUPCAKES

*These tasty little cakes show off how versatile our basic cake recipes are. The chocolate cream–filled cupcakes are an updated version of the cupcakes our moms packed into our lunchboxes. The lemon cupcakes are a special treat—white cakes filled with lemon curd, perfect for afternoon tea.*

## CHOCOLATE CREAM–FILLED CUPCAKES

24 DEVIL'S FOOD CUPCAKES (PAGE 67)          1 RECIPE CHOCOLATE GANACHE
½ RECIPE BUTTERCREAM FROSTING              (PAGE 123)
(PAGE 120)

ASSEMBLY:

1.  Prepare all the ingredients.

2.  Fill a pastry bag with buttercream frosting. Carefully insert the tip of the pastry bag into the cupcake. Squeeze the bag and release frosting into the center of the cupcake. Repeat until all cupcakes are filled.

3.  Use a spatula to spread ganache onto the tops of the cupcakes. With buttercream frosting, pipe a small star design on top of each cupcake. Refrigerate until serving. Serve at room temperature.

YIELD: 24 CUPCAKES

## LEMON CUPCAKES

20 WHITE LAYER CAKE CUPCAKES               1 RECIPE LEMON CURD FILLING
(PAGE 64)                                  (PAGE 80)
                                           CONFECTIONERS' SUGAR FOR DUSTING

ASSEMBLY:

1.  Using a paring knife, scoop out the top of the cupcakes, about ½ inch deep. Set tops aside.

**2.** Using a teaspoon, fill cupcake bottoms with lemon curd filling. If the filling sticks to your fingers, dip your fingers in water to help release the filling from the teaspoon. Place tops back on top of filling. Press gently. Dust tops with confectioners' sugar. Refrigerate. Serve at room temperature.

YIELD: 20 CUPCAKES

# BUTTERCREAM FROSTING

*This is a rich, traditional frosting suitable for any occasion. If you want to do fancier decorating, be sure to make 1½ recipes or double the recipe for additional frosting.*

½ POUND BUTTER, SOFTENED             1 TEASPOON VANILLA EXTRACT

6 CUPS CONFECTIONERS' SUGAR          2 EGG WHITES

1. In an electric mixer on low speed, cream the butter and 4 cups of the confectioners' sugar. Add vanilla. Gradually add the remaining 2 cups of confectioners' sugar and egg whites. Scrape down the sides of the bowl.

2. Beat on high speed until light in color and texture, about 5 minutes.

3. Use immediately or cover in an airtight container and refrigerate. Bring frosting to room temperature before using. If necessary, thin with a few teaspoons of water for easier spreading.

YIELD: ENOUGH TO FILL, FROST, AND PIPE TOP AND BOTTOM BORDERS AROUND A
TWO-LAYER 9-INCH ROUND CAKE

# CHOCOLATE BUTTERCREAM FROSTING

*This rich frosting is perfect on our Banana Sour Cream Cake, Chip & Ernie's Cake,
Turtle Cake, or Chocolate Strawberry Valentine Cake.*

½ POUND BUTTER, SOFTENED

1 CUP COCOA

6 CUPS CONFECTIONERS' SUGAR

½ CUP COLD BREWED COFFEE

1. In an electric mixer, cream the butter. Add cocoa and 4 cups of the confectioners' sugar. Beat on low speed until blended. Add remaining confectioners' sugar and coffee. Beat on medium high for 3 to 4 minutes, or until smooth and well blended.

2. Use immediately or store refrigerated in an airtight container. Bring frosting to room temperature before using. If necessary, thin with a few teaspoons of water for easier spreading.

YIELD: ENOUGH TO FILL AND FROST A TWO-LAYER 9-INCH ROUND CAKE

---

◆ **CAKE DECORATING PRACTICE** ◆

A GOOD WAY TO PRACTICE BORDERS IS TO PIPE THEM ONTO A COOKIE SHEET LINED WITH WAXED PAPER. AFTER PIPING A FEW ROWS, SCRAPE UP THE FROSTING AND REPEAT AGAIN. PRACTICE WILL REALLY HELP YOU REGULATE THE AMOUNT OF PRESSURE NEEDED TO ADD TO THE BAG TO GET A BORDER OF THE DESIRED SIZE. YOU CAN ALSO PRACTICE ALONG THE EDGE OF A CAKE PAN, TURNED UPSIDE DOWN. OR YOU CAN ALWAYS JUST BAKE A CAKE—AND REWARD YOURSELF WITH A SLICE AT THE END OF THE PRACTICE SESSION.

---

# WHIPPED CREAM FROSTING

*This fresh and versatile frosting is the perfect complement to cakes filled with fresh fruit or custard fillings. Our version is slightly sweetened. If you prefer a sweeter cream, just increase the sugar.*

2 CUPS HEAVY CREAM                    ¼ CUP SUGAR

In an electric mixer with wire whisk attachment, beat cream into peaks, 2 to 3 minutes. Add sugar and whip until stiff. Use immediately.

YIELD: 4 CUPS, ENOUGH TO FILL AND FROST A TWO-LAYER 9-INCH POUND CAKE

# CREAM CHEESE FROSTING

*This rich and flavorful frosting complements spicier cakes like carrot, spice cake, amaretto, apple, and gingerbread.*

16 OUNCES CREAM CHEESE,              6 CUPS CONFECTIONERS' SUGAR
SOFTENED

¼ POUND BUTTER, SOFTENED

1. In an electric mixer, blend together cream cheese and butter. Whip on medium-high speed for 3 to 4 minutes, or until fluffy.

2. On low speed, gradually add confectioners' sugar until well blended and smooth. Use immediately or store, refrigerated, in an airtight container. Let frosting come to room temperature before using.

YIELD: ENOUGH TO FILL AND FROST A TWO-LAYER 9-INCH ROUND CAKE

# CHOCOLATE GANACHE

*This rich chocolate glaze is poured over a chocolate frosted cake for a dark, smooth appearance and a rich flavor. Be sure that your chocolate is finely ground. The finer the chocolate, the easier it will blend with the hot cream. It works best when used to coat a cake that has a thin base coat of chocolate buttercream frosting.*

**8 OUNCES SEMISWEET CHOCOLATE**     **½ CUP HEAVY CREAM**

1. Process chocolate in food processor until finely ground.

2. Place processed chocolate in a medium mixing bowl.

3. Heat heavy cream in a small saucepan over medium heat. Heat until just about boiling, stirring constantly with a wooden spoon. Pour hot cream over chocolate and stir until well blended and smooth. Cool to lukewarm before using. Store refrigerated in an airtight container. To reheat, heat in a double boiler over simmering water. Stir until smooth.

**YIELD: ENOUGH TO COVER ONE 9-INCH LAYER CAKE, 12 MINI LOAF CAKES, OR 24 CUPCAKES**

# LEMON OR LIME
# SEVEN-MINUTE FROSTING

*This frosting gets its name from the amount of time you need to whip it. It has a light
meringue quality and looks great when simply "stippled" into small peaks with a metal
spatula. The pure white mounds of frosting always remind me of big fluffy clouds.
Be careful—it's easy to get distracted when whipping this frosting.
I suggest setting a timer before you begin.
Adding lemon or lime juice to this recipe instead of the traditional water gives the
frosting a flavor burst that complements the cakes and fillings it's paired with.*

1½ CUPS SUGAR

⅓ CUP LEMON OR LIME JUICE

2 EGG WHITES

¼ TEASPOON CREAM OF TARTAR

¼ TEASPOON SALT

1. Combine sugar, lemon or lime juice, egg whites, cream of tartar, and salt in the
   top of a double boiler. Beat with an electric mixer until blended. Continue mixing on high speed over boiling water until stiff peaks form, 7 to 10 minutes.

2. Remove frosting from the water and continue beating until cool and thick
   enough to spread, another 4 to 5 minutes. Use immediately.

YIELD: ENOUGH FROSTING TO COVER A 9-INCH LAYER CAKE

VARIATION:

## ALMOND SEVEN-MINUTE FROSTING
Omit lemon or lime juice and add 1½ teaspoons almond extract.

# WEDDING CAKE ASSEMBLY

# INDEX